Name:

About the Artist's Fun-Schooling Journal

This 300-page journal is designed for homeschoolers interested in art and drawing. It covers several required subjects while focusing on the student's passion. The student will work through this learning handbook using resources from the Internet, local library and family bookshelf. The Artist's Fun-Schooling Journal is perfect for artists of all abilities, ages 9+, or younger with assistance. The book also includes reading, writing, history, math, and more, so a student can approach learning as a whole, while studying art and drawing. Students will work through Art Challenge prompts, draw nature, and color beautiful coloring pages.

To complete this guided learning journal students need access to library books and films/documentaries easily found online. This curriculum can be used daily for an intensive art units study lasting about six weeks or once a week to make it last all school year.

Thinking Tree Learning Levels: B2 & C1, ideal for ages 9+ (even adults!), younger children with assistance. Excellent companion journal to our "Teach Yourself to Draw" resources.

This book uses the Open Dyslexic font for easier reading for Dyslexic students.

Topics Covered Include:

- Planning & setting priorities
- Artist Biographies
- Reading & writing
- Film study
- Art History
- Art challenges
- Comics
- Math practice
- Drawing Games

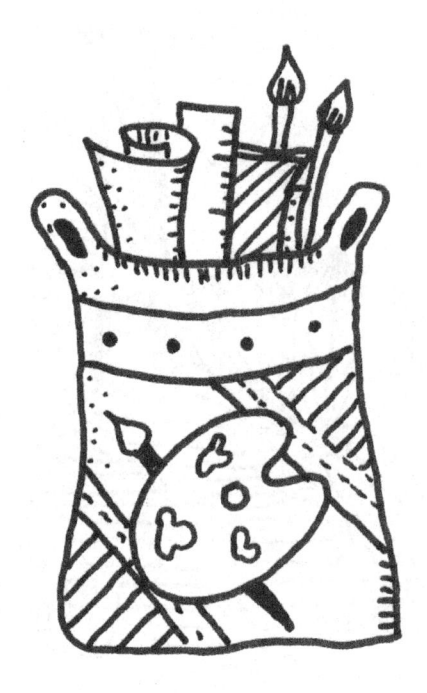

The Thinking Tree

THE ARTIST'S FUN-SCHOOLING JOURNAL

Homeschooling Curriculum Handbook

For Students Majoring in ART

Anna Miriam Brown

Sarah Janisse Brown

Joshua William Brown

Copyright 2019

The Thinking Tree, LLC

FunSchooling.com

Instructions

Draw or list six things you want to learn about or art skills you want to develop:

1.

2.

3.

4.

5.

6.

Action Steps:

1. Go to the library, your bookshelf, or a bookstore.
2. Bring home a stack of six to nine books about these topics or skills.
3. Gather your supplies and get creative!

Supplies Needed:

You will need pencils, art supplies (colored pencils or gel pens work best), and films/documentaries.

Choose Your Books

Pick out six to nine different books that will help you study art.

Draw the covers and titles here:

Plans & Priorities

Date:_____

To-do List:
_____
_____
_____
_____

A Quote:
_____
_____
_____
_____

My Goals:
_____
_____
_____
_____

My Plans:
_____
_____
_____
_____

Notes:
_____
_____
_____
_____

Relax & Be Creative

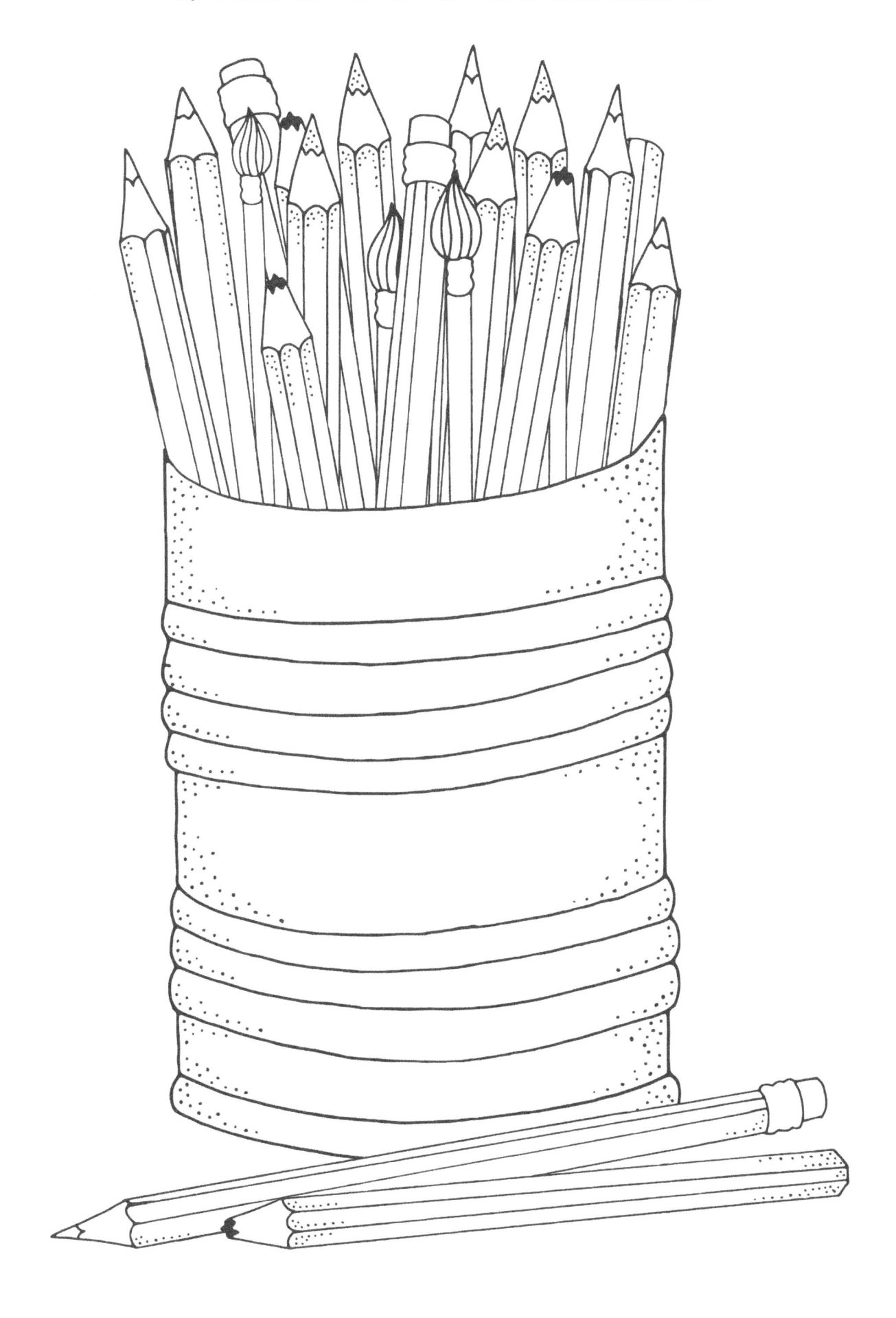

Drawing & Reading Time!

Choose a few books from your stack to focus on today.
Write down and draw what inspires you.
(Set a timer for 1 hour)

Study an Artist
From Italy

Name: _____

What is this artist known for?
_____
_____
_____

What makes their artwork unique?
_____
_____
_____
_____
_____

Random fact about this artist or their art:
_____
_____

Write a short biography about this artist:
_____
_____
_____
_____
_____
_____
_____
_____
_____
_____
_____
_____
_____
_____

Design a postage stamp to commemorate this person

Art Challenge

On this page, draw a realistic drawing of something in the room with you. Draw the same thing as a cartoon on the next page.

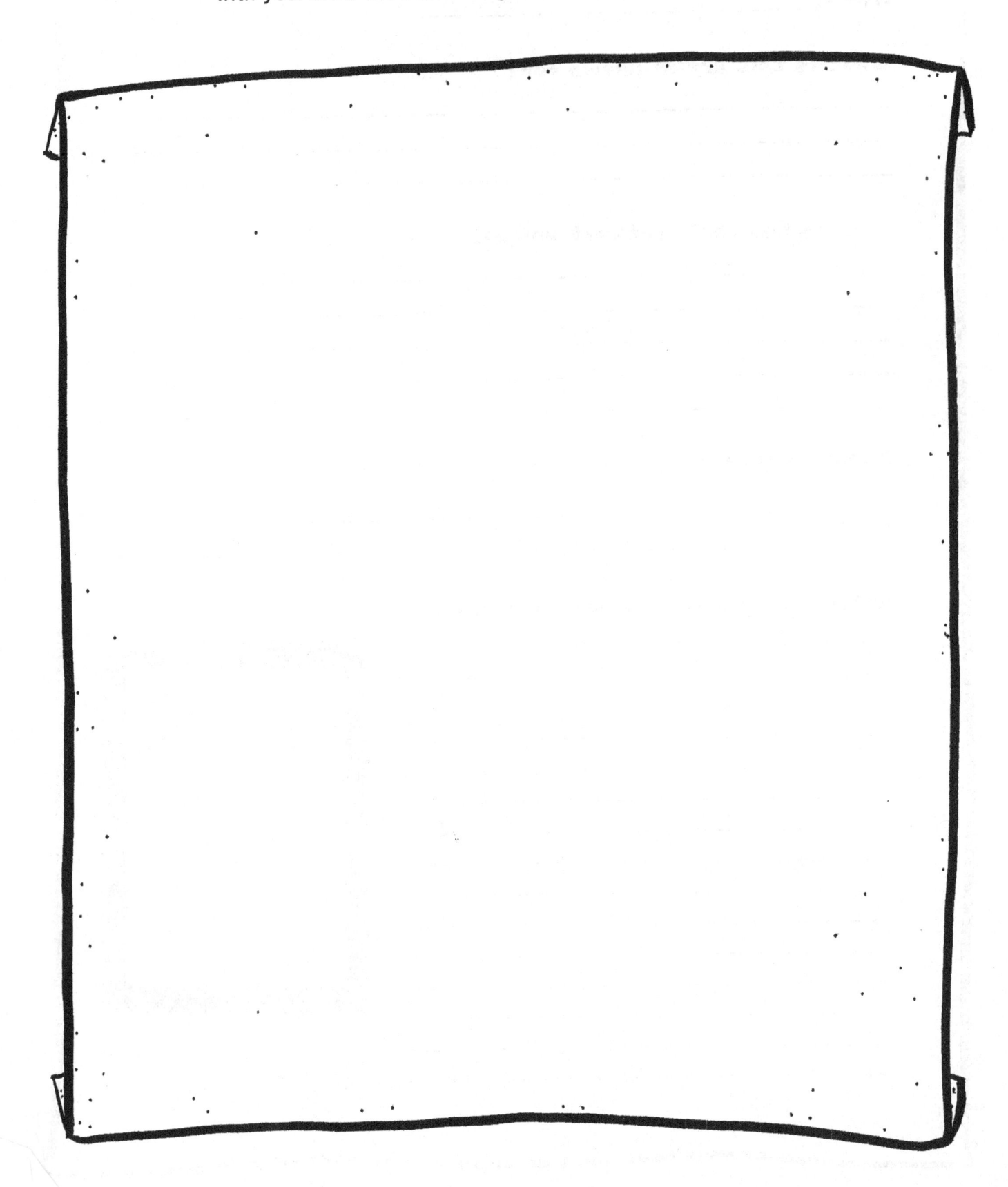

Math & Design Practice

Use this page for math practice, graphic design, pixel art, and creative measurements.

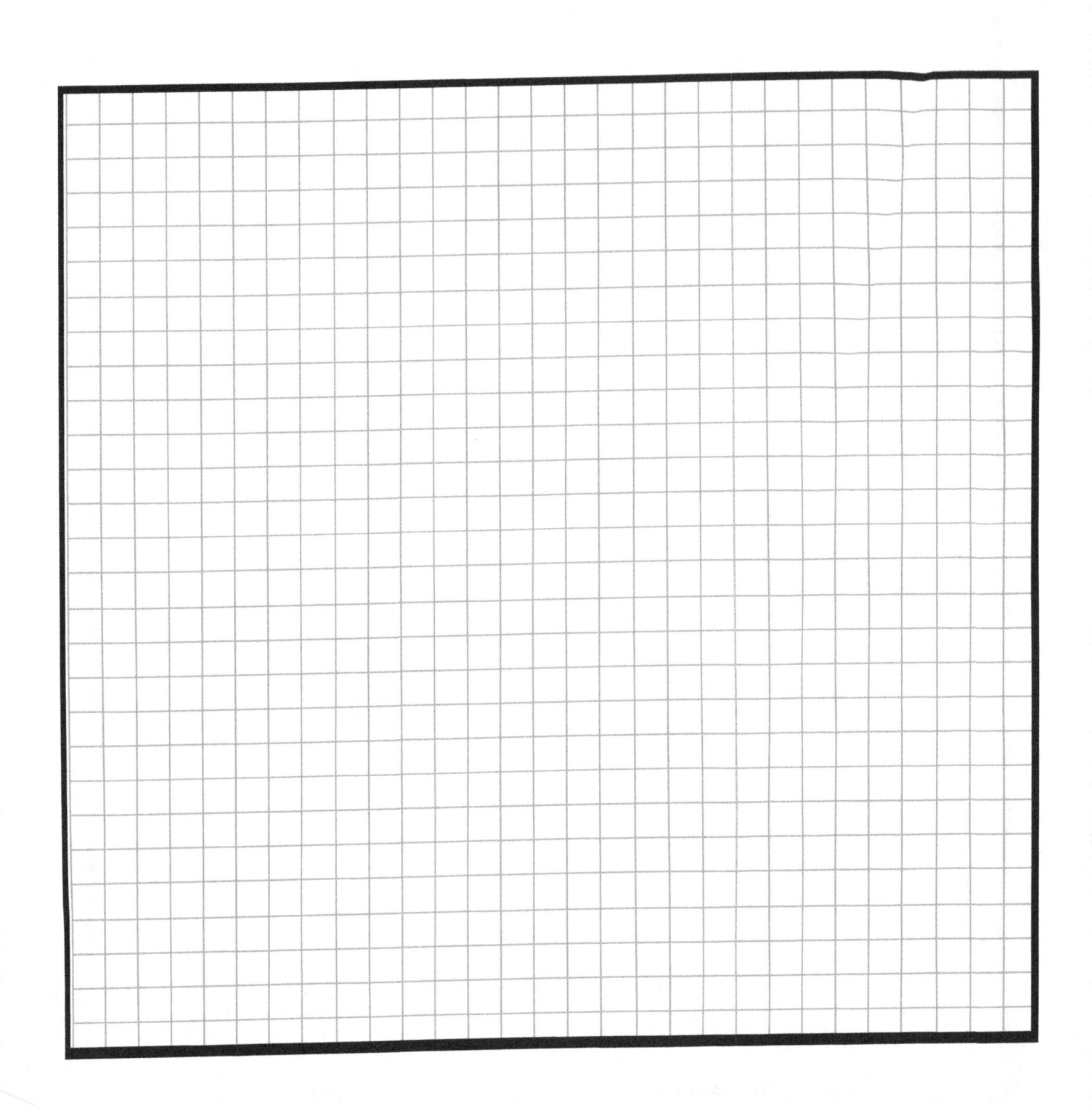

Nature Study

Take this book outside and draw anything and everything that inspires you.

Plans & Priorities

Date:_____

To-do List:
_____
_____
_____
_____
_____

A Quote:
_____
_____
_____
_____

My Goals:
_____
_____
_____
_____

My Plans:
_____
_____
_____
_____
_____

Notes:
_____
_____
_____
_____

Relax & Be Creative

Drawing & Reading Time!

Choose a few books from your stack to focus on today.
Write down and draw what inspires you.
(Set a timer for 1 hour)

Study an Artist
From the 1500's

Name:_____

What is this artist known for?
_____
_____
_____

What makes their artwork unique?
_____
_____
_____
_____
_____

Random fact about this artist or their art:
_____
_____

Write a short biography about this artist:
_____
_____
_____
_____
_____
_____
_____
_____
_____
_____
_____
_____

Design a postage stamp to commemorate this person

Screen Time

Watch a high-quality film, video, tutorial or documentary.

Title_____

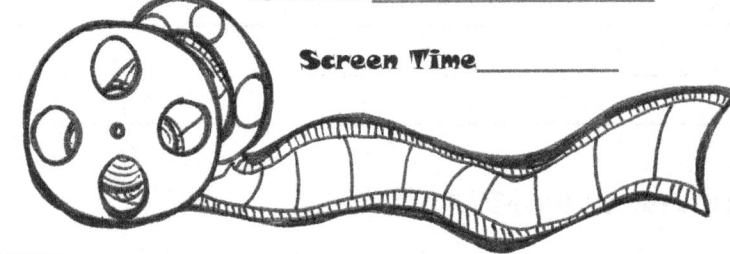

Screen Time_____

Producer_____

Actors_____

_____

_____

_____

Draw it

Pause the video and draw your favorite scene from the film.

Worst

Bad

Awful

Ok

Nice

Great

Best

Make a Comic

Based on the video you watched during screen time.

Title_____

Art Challenge

Sketch your favorite animal in a few different positions, perhaps sitting, sleeping, running, or swimming.

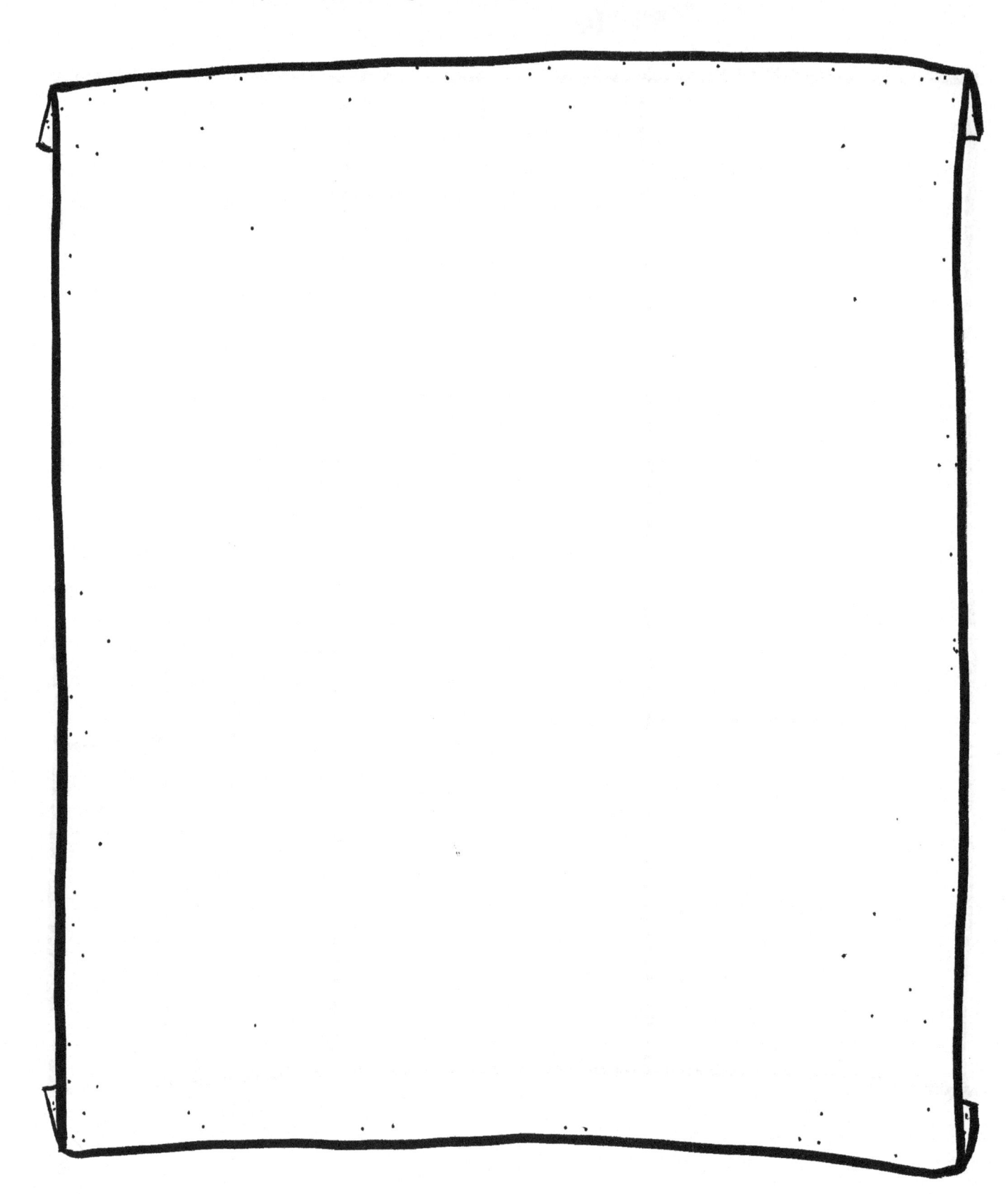

Math & Design Practice

Use this page for math practice, graphic design, pixel art, and creative measurements.

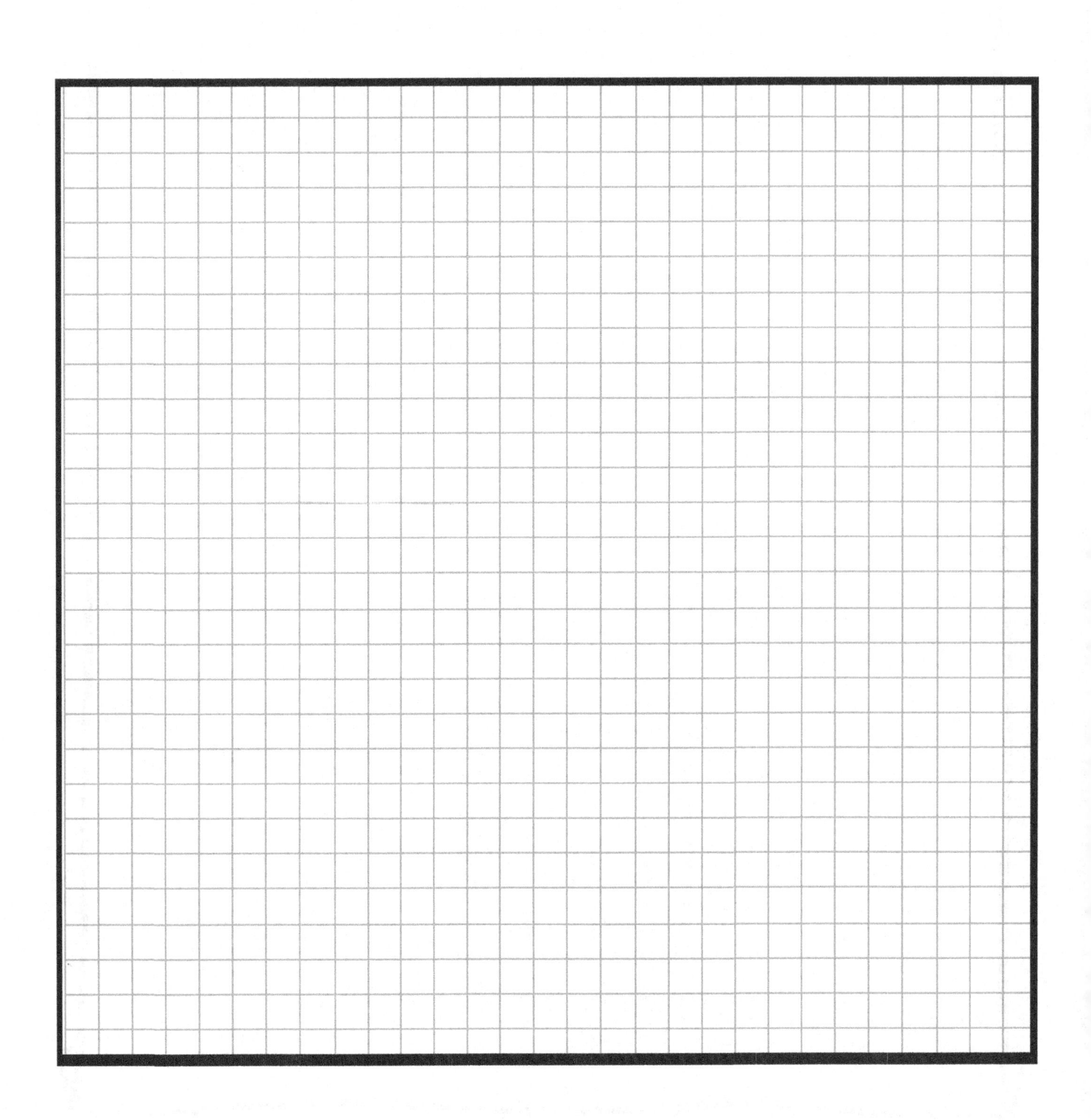

Nature Study

Take this book outside and draw anything and everything that inspires you.

Plans & Priorities

Date:_____

To-do List:
_____
_____
_____
_____
_____

A Quote:
_____
_____
_____
_____

My Goals:
_____
_____
_____
_____

My Plans:
_____
_____
_____
_____
_____

Notes:
_____
_____
_____
_____

Relax & Be Creative

Drawing & Reading Time!

Choose a few books from your stack to focus on today.
Write down and draw what inspires you.
(Set a timer for 1 hour)

Study an Artist
From England

Name:_____

What is this artist known for?
_____
_____
_____

What makes their artwork unique?
_____
_____
_____
_____
_____

Random fact about this artist or their art:
_____
_____

Write a short biography about this artist:
_____
_____
_____
_____
_____
_____
_____
_____
_____
_____
_____

Design a postage stamp to commemorate this person

Screen Time

Watch a high-quality film, video, tutorial or documentary.

Title_____

Screen Time_____

Producer_____

Actors_____
_____
_____
_____

Draw it

Pause the video and draw your favorite scene from the film.

Worst

Bad

Awful

Ok

Nice

Great

Best

Make a Comic

Based on the video you watched during screen time.

Title_____

Art Challenge

Draw a bakery. Look at a photo of a real bakery to inspire you.

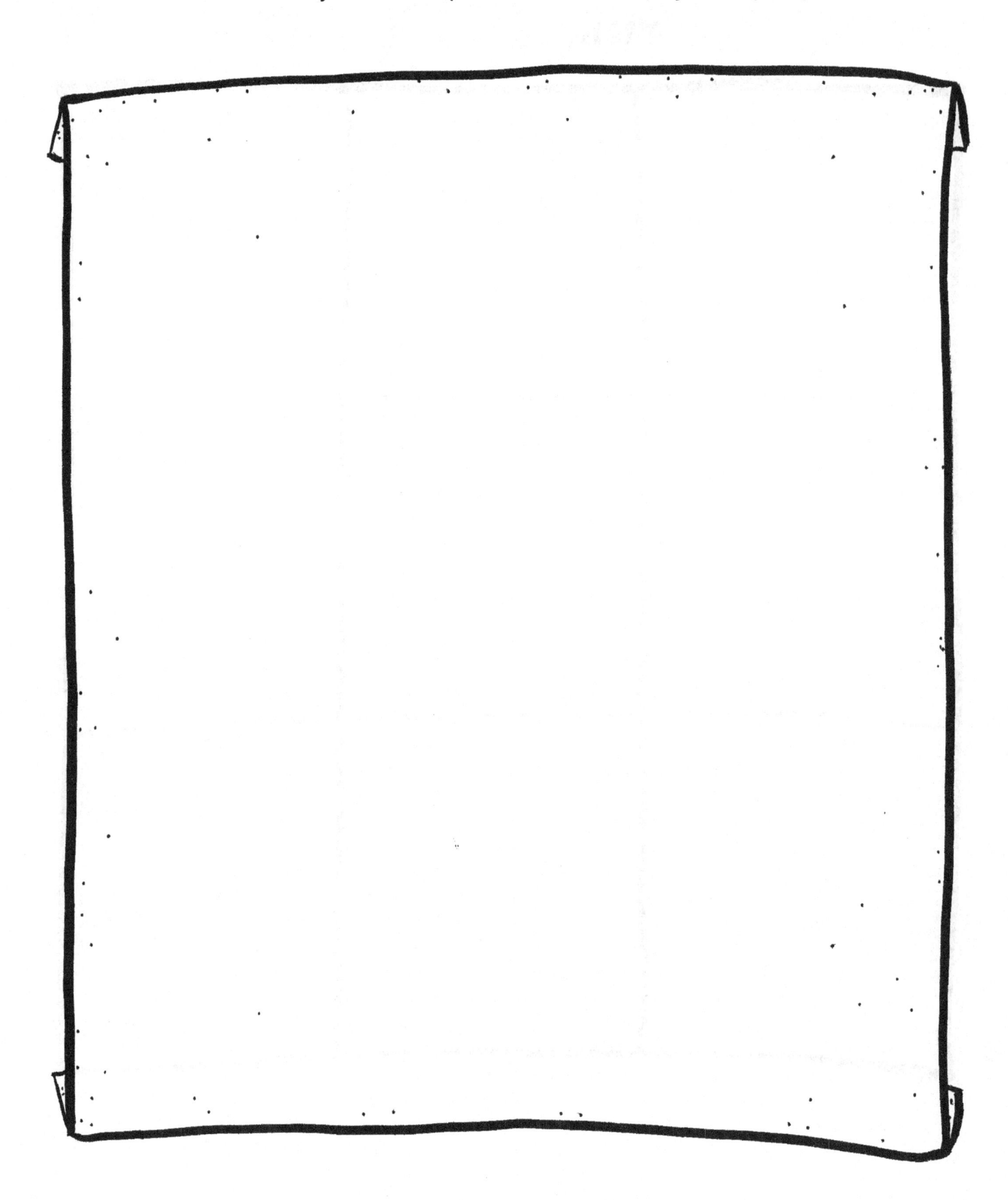

Math & Design Practice

Use this page for math practice, graphic design, pixel art, and creative measurements.

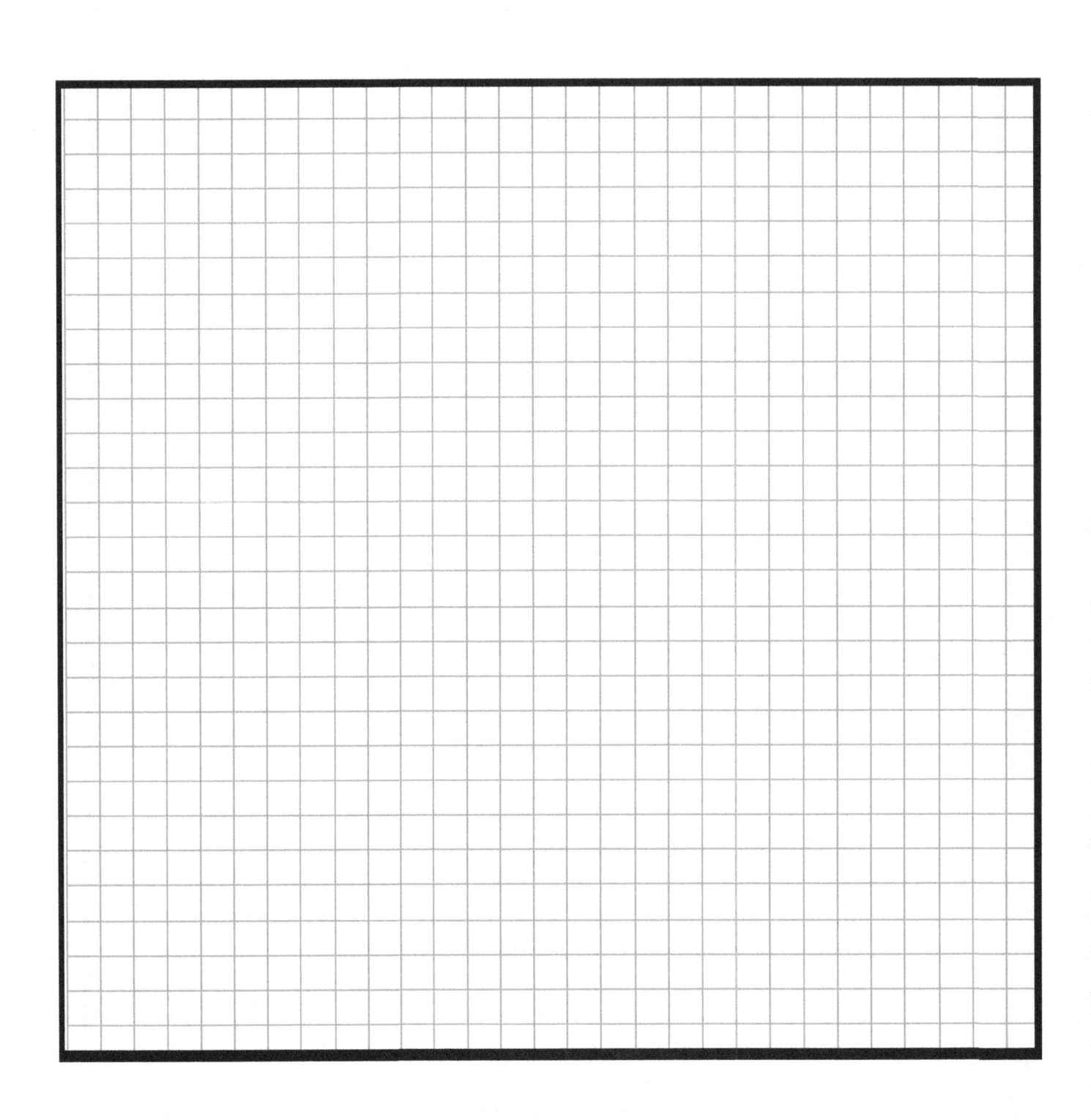

Nature Study

Take this book outside and draw anything and everything that inspires you.

Plans & Priorities

Date: _____

To-do List:
_____
_____
_____
_____
_____

A Quote:
_____
_____
_____
_____

My Goals:
_____
_____
_____
_____

My Plans:
_____
_____
_____
_____

Notes:
_____
_____
_____
_____

Relax & Be Creative

Drawing & Reading Time!

Choose a few books from your stack to focus on today.
Write down and draw what inspires you.
(Set a timer for 1 hour)

Study an Artist
From the USA

Name: _____

What is this artist known for?
_____
_____
_____

What makes their artwork unique?
_____
_____
_____
_____
_____

Random fact about this artist or their art:
_____
_____

Write a short biography about this artist:
_____
_____
_____
_____
_____
_____
_____
_____
_____
_____
_____
_____
_____

Design a postage stamp to commemorate this person

Screen Time

Watch a high-quality film, video, tutorial or documentary.

Title_____

Screen Time_____

Producer_____

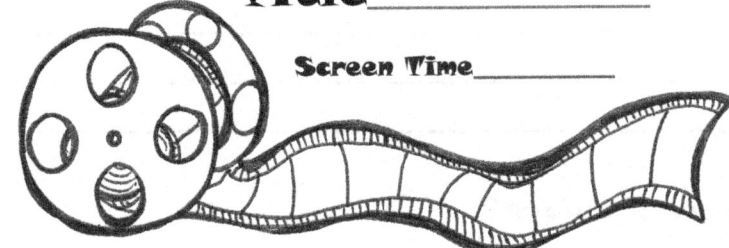

Actors_____

_____

_____

_____

_____

Draw it

Pause the video and draw your favorite scene from the film.

Worst

Bad

Awful

Ok

Nice

Great

Best

Make a Comic

Based on the video you watched during screen time.

Title_____

Art Challenge

Draw a pair of identical twins
that are nothing like each other.

Math & Design Practice

Use this page for math practice, graphic design, pixel art, and creative measurements.

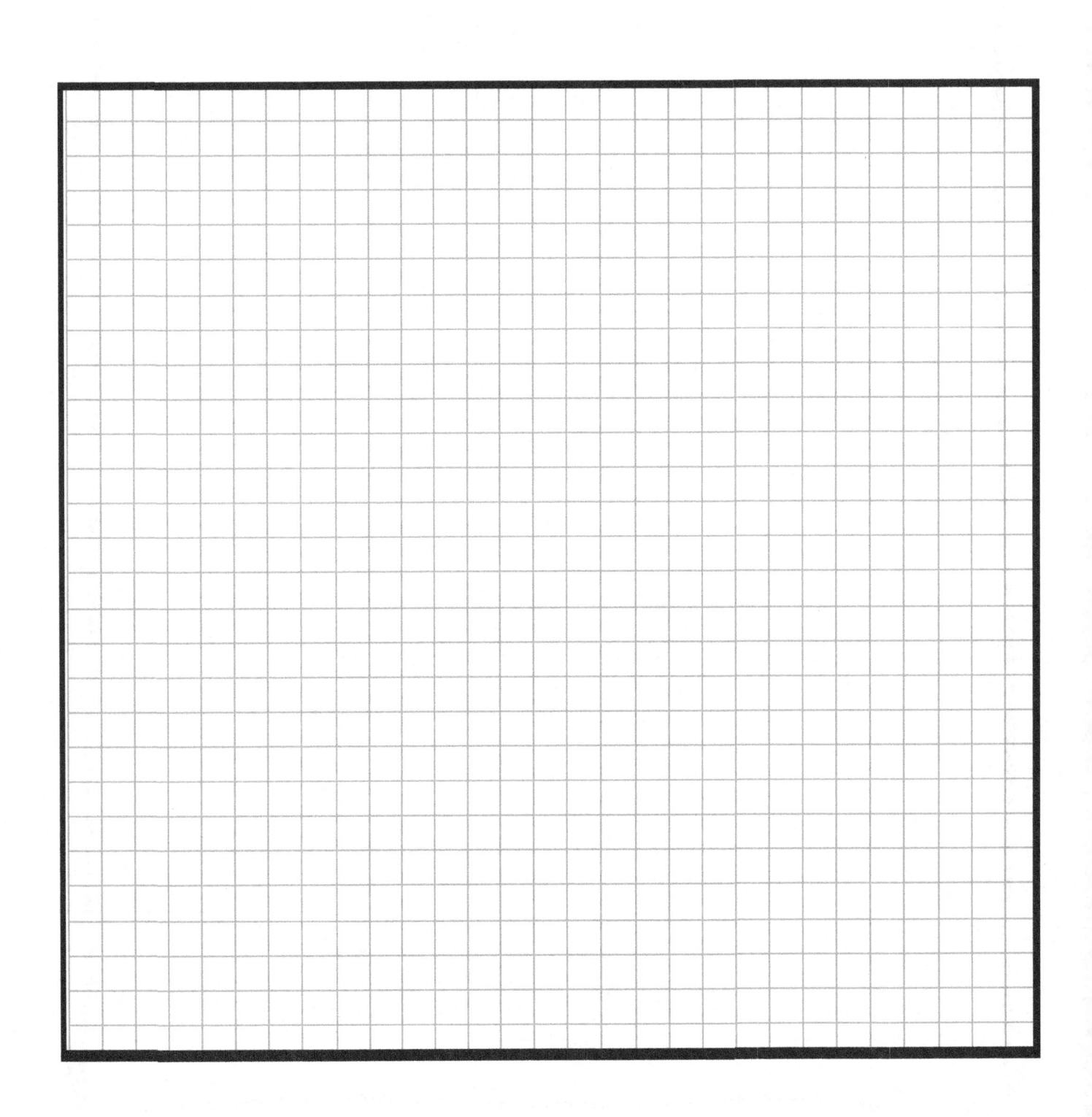

Nature Study

Take this book outside and draw anything and everything that inspires you.

Plans & Priorities

Date:_____

To-do List:
_____
_____
_____
_____
_____

A Quote:
_____
_____
_____
_____
_____

My Goals:
_____
_____
_____
_____

My Plans:
_____
_____
_____
_____

Notes:
_____
_____
_____
_____

Relax & Be Creative

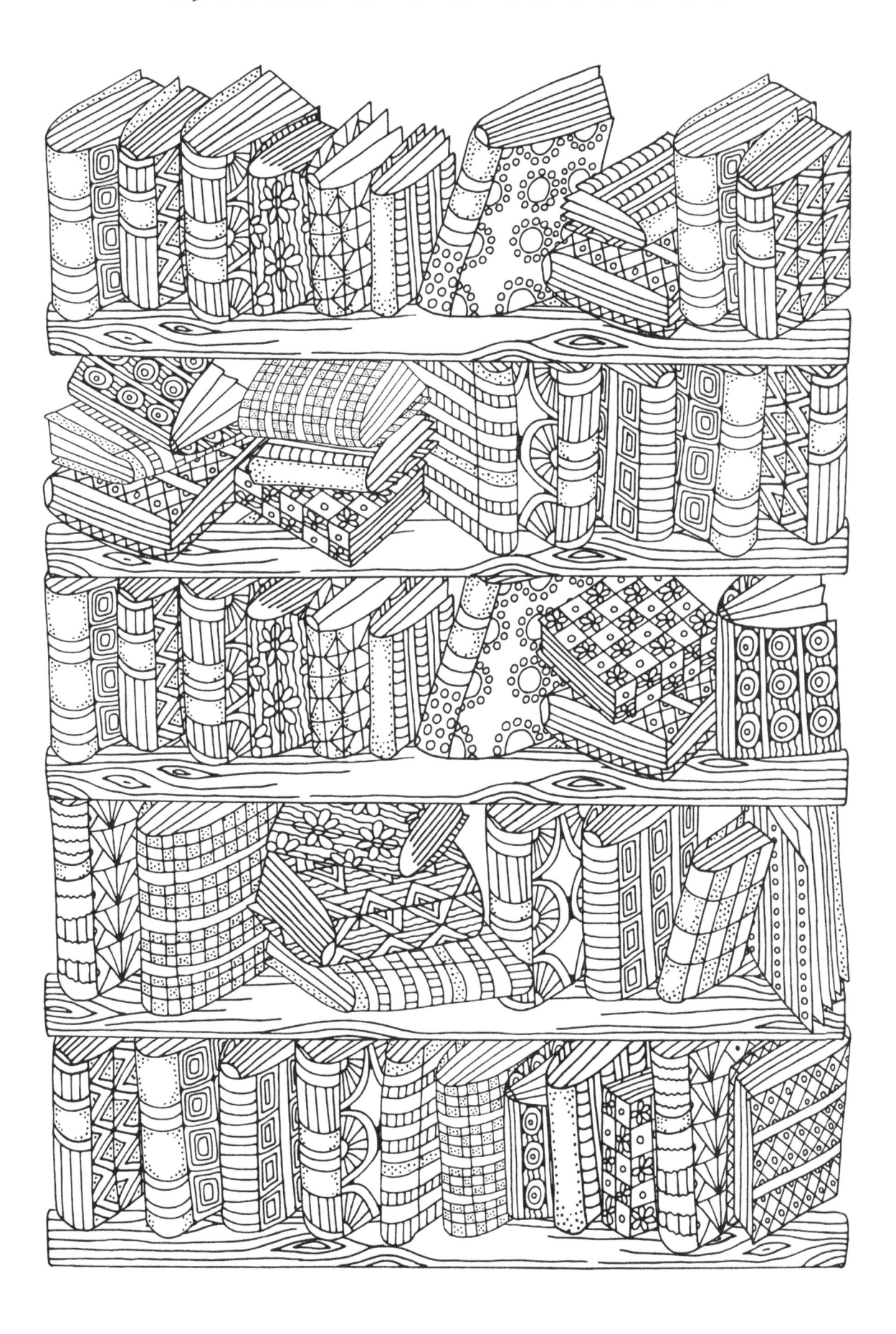

Drawing & Reading Time!

Choose a few books from your stack to focus on today.
Write down and draw what inspires you.
(Set a timer for 1 hour)

Study an Artist
You Choose!

Name: _____

What is this artist known for?
_____
_____
_____

What makes their artwork unique?
_____
_____
_____
_____
_____

Random fact about this artist or their art:
_____
_____

Write a short biography about this artist:
_____
_____
_____
_____
_____
_____
_____
_____
_____
_____
_____
_____

Design a postage stamp to commemorate this person

Screen Time

Watch a high-quality film, video, tutorial or documentary.

Title_____

Screen Time_____

Producer_____

Actors_____

_____
_____
_____

Draw it

Pause the video and draw your favorite scene from the film.

Worst

Bad

Awful

Ok

Nice

Great

Best

Make a Comic

Based on the video you watched during screen time.

Title_____

Art Challenge

Close your eyes and draw what you feel like drawing.
Open your eyes and add details to the design.

Math & Design Practice

Use this page for math practice, graphic design, pixel art, and creative measurements.

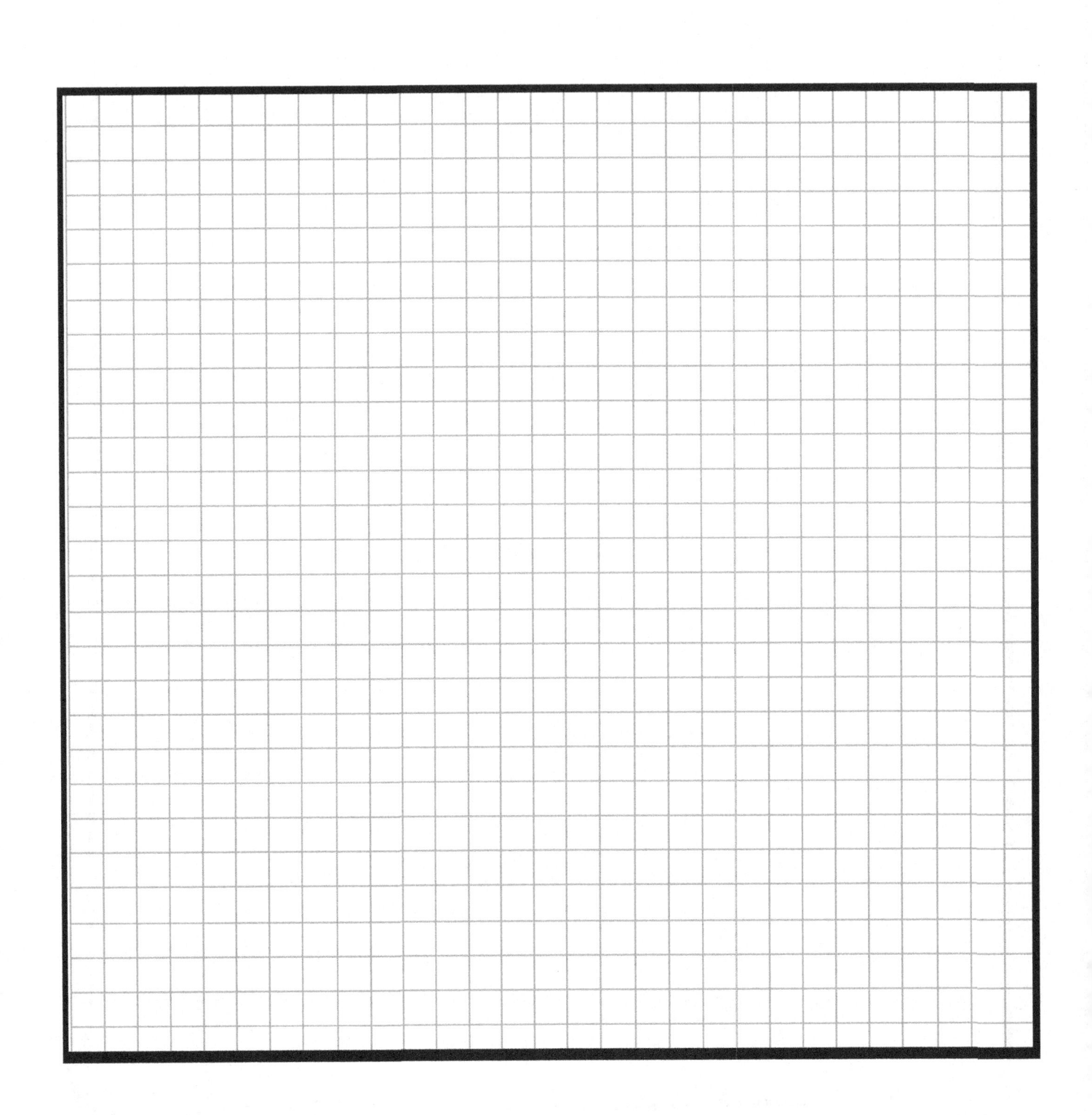

Nature Study

Take this book outside and draw anything and everything that inspires you.

Plans & Priorities

Date:_____

To-do List:
_____
_____
_____
_____
_____

A Quote:
_____
_____
_____
_____
_____

My Goals:
_____
_____
_____
_____
_____

My Plans:
_____
_____
_____
_____
_____

Notes:
_____
_____
_____
_____

Relax & Be Creative

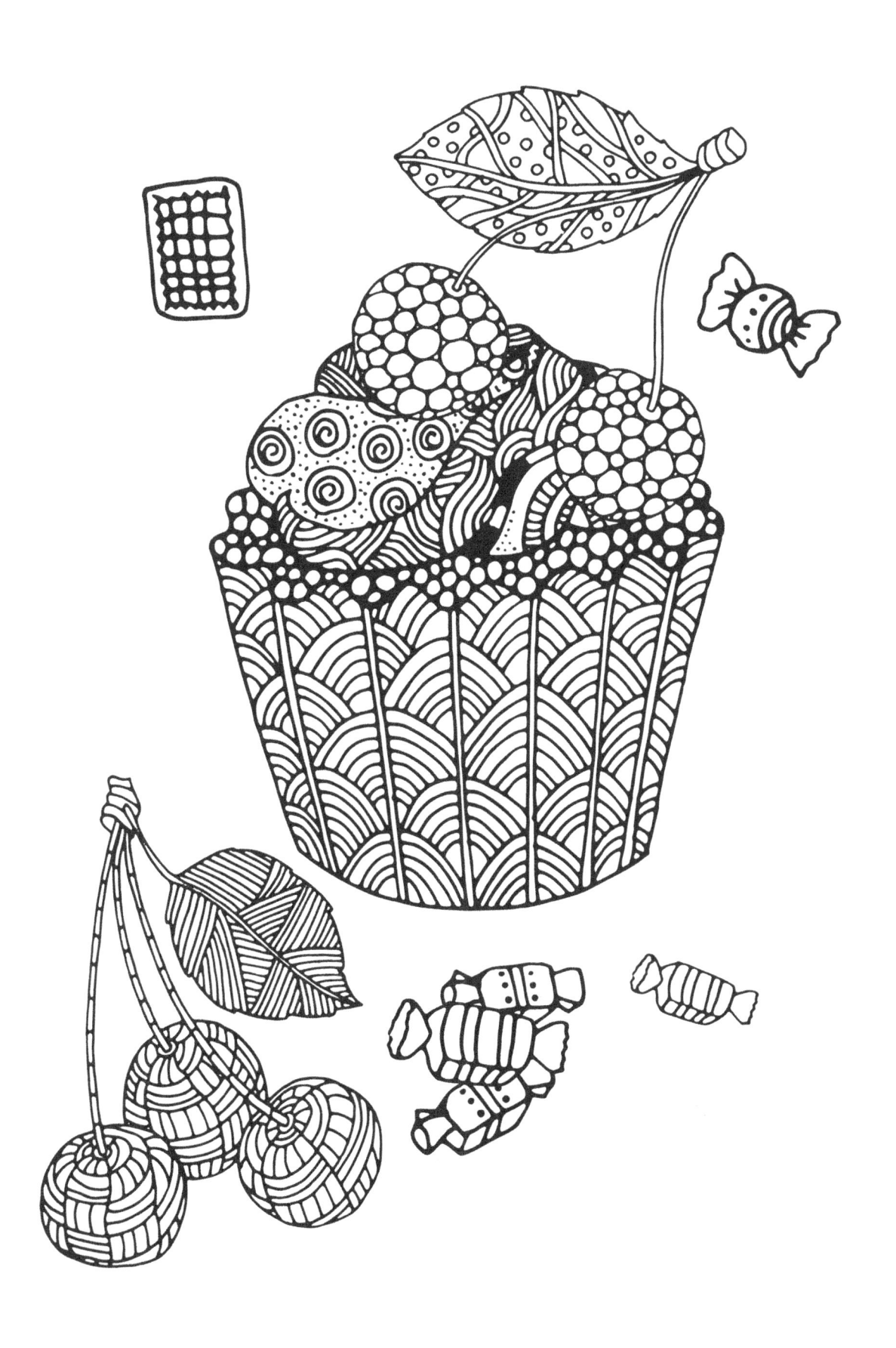

Drawing & Reading Time!

Choose a few books from your stack to focus on today.
Write down and draw what inspires you.
(Set a timer for 1 hour)

Study an Artist
From China

Name: _____

What is this artist known for?
_____
_____
_____

What makes their artwork unique?
_____
_____
_____
_____
_____

Random fact about this artist or their art:
_____
_____

Write a short biography about this artist:
_____
_____
_____
_____
_____
_____
_____
_____
_____
_____
_____
_____

Design a postage stamp to commemorate this person

Screen Time

Watch a high-quality film, video, tutorial or documentary.

Title_____

Screen Time_____

Producer_____

Actors_____

_____

_____

_____

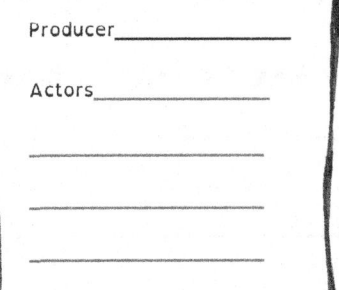

Draw it

Pause the video and draw your favorite scene from the film.

Worst

Bad

Awful

Ok

Nice

Great

Best

Make a Comic

Based on the video you watched during screen time.

Title_____

Art Challenge

Use pencils to copy the sketches of a well known artist such as Norman Rockwell or Leonardo DaVinci.

Math & Design Practice

Use this page for math practice, graphic design, pixel art, and creative measurements.

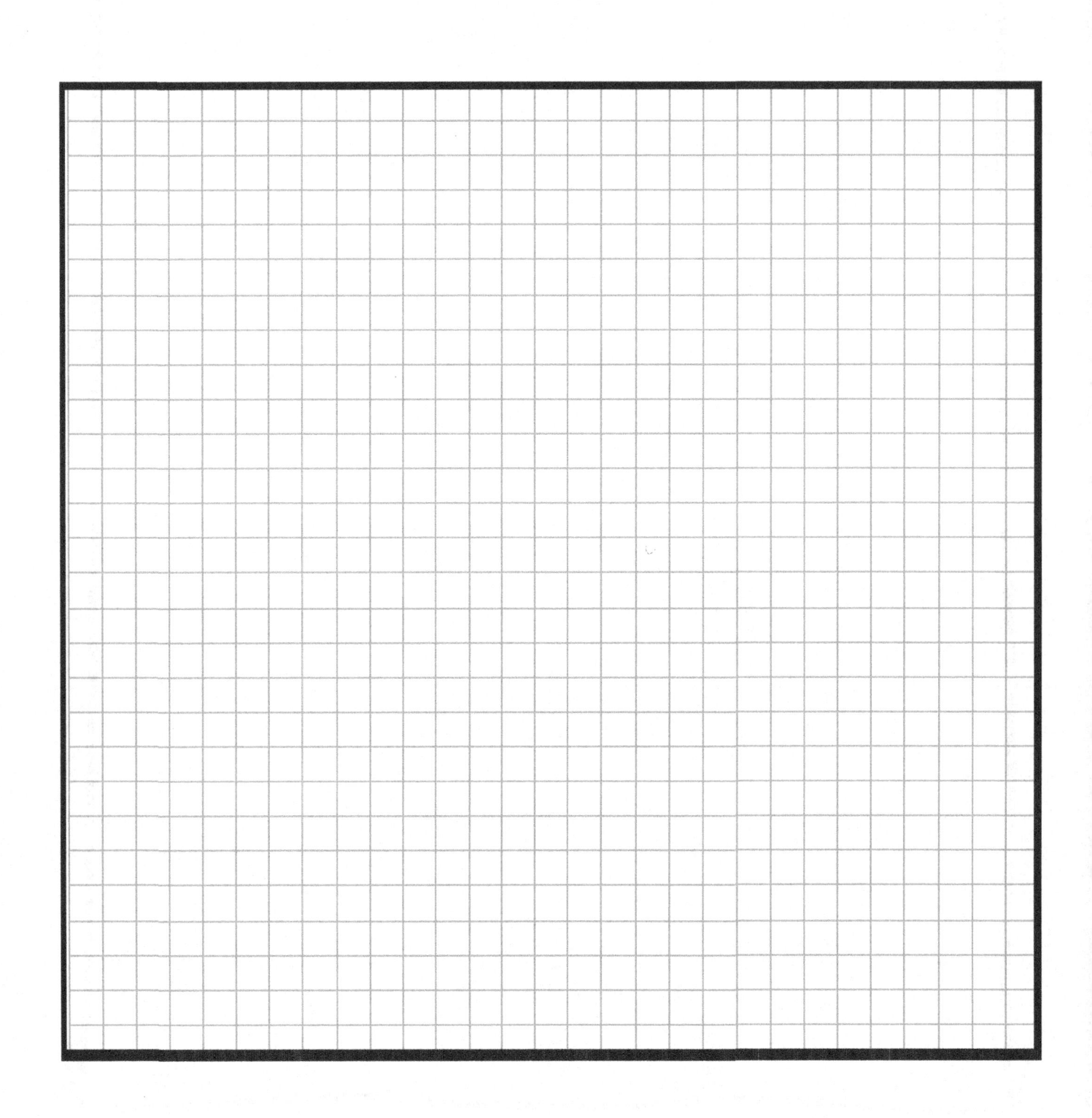

Nature Study

Take this book outside and draw anything and everything that inspires you.

Plans & Priorities

Date: _____

To-do List:
_____
_____
_____
_____
_____

A Quote:
_____
_____
_____
_____
_____

My Goals:
_____
_____
_____
_____
_____

My Plans:
_____
_____
_____
_____
_____

Notes:
_____
_____
_____
_____

Relax & Be Creative

Drawing & Reading Time!

Choose a few books from your stack to focus on today.
Write down and draw what inspires you.
(Set a timer for 1 hour)

Study an Artist
From France

Name: _____

What is this artist known for?
_____
_____
_____

What makes their artwork unique?
_____
_____
_____
_____
_____

Random fact about this artist or their art:
_____
_____

Write a short biography about this artist:
_____
_____
_____
_____
_____
_____
_____
_____
_____
_____
_____

Design a postage stamp to commemorate this person

Art Challenge

Draw your best friend without looking at a picture.
On the next page, draw them while looking at a picture.

Math & Design Practice

Use this page for math practice, graphic design, pixel art, and creative measurements.

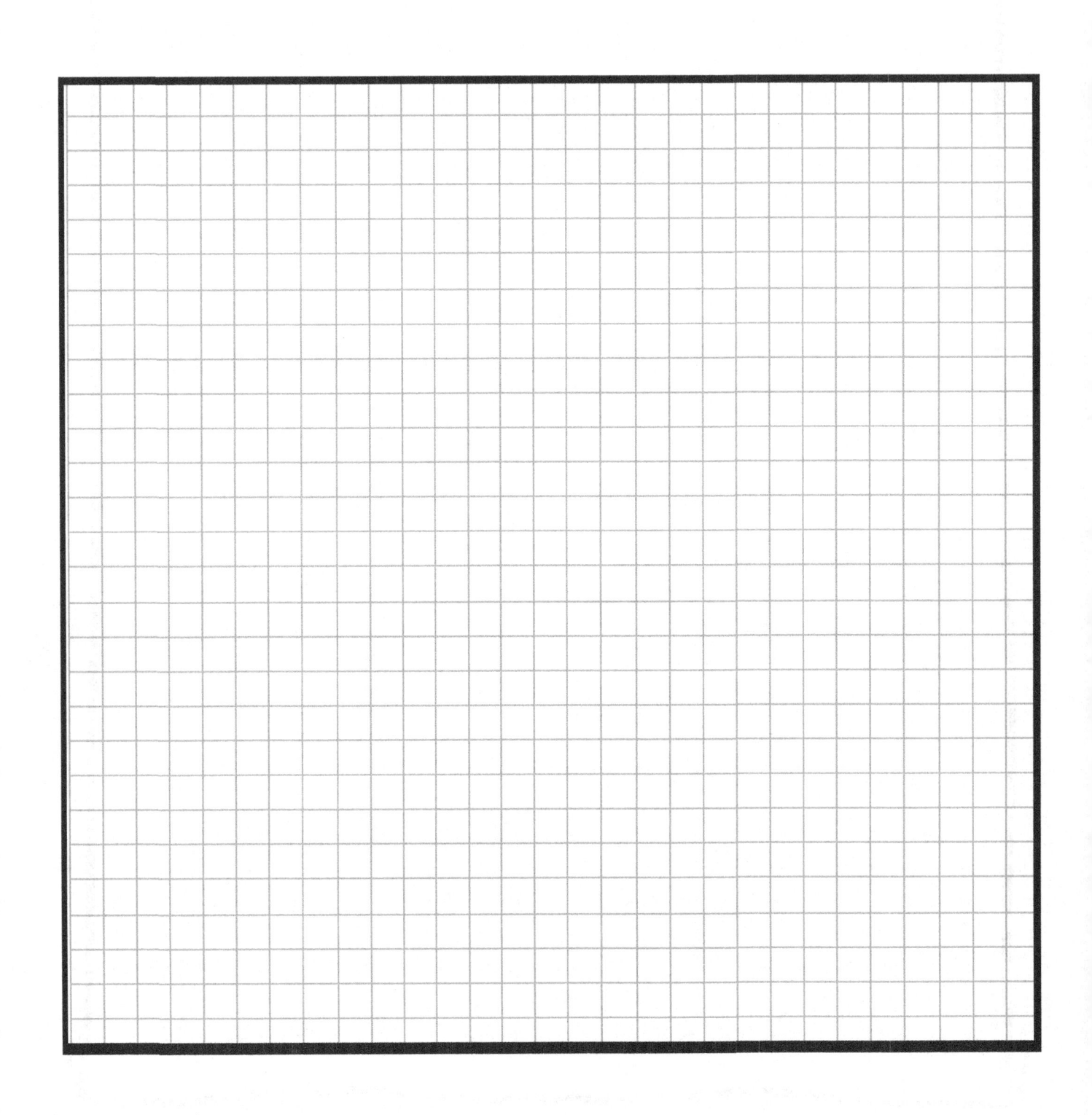

Nature Study

Take this book outside and draw anything and everything that inspires you.

Plans & Priorities

Date:_____

To-do List:
_____
_____
_____
_____
_____

A Quote:
_____
_____
_____
_____
_____

My Goals:
_____
_____
_____
_____
_____

My Plans:
_____
_____
_____
_____
_____

Notes:
_____
_____
_____
_____

Relax & Be Creative

Drawing & Reading Time!

Choose a few books from your stack to focus on today.
Write down and draw what inspires you.
(Set a timer for 1 hour)

Study an Artist
From the 1600's

Name:_____

What is this artist known for?
_____
_____
_____

What makes their artwork unique?
_____
_____
_____
_____
_____

Random fact about this artist or their art:
_____
_____

Write a short biography about this artist:
_____
_____
_____
_____
_____
_____
_____
_____
_____
_____
_____
_____

Design a postage stamp to commemorate this person

Screen Time

Watch a high-quality film, video, tutorial or documentary.

Title_____

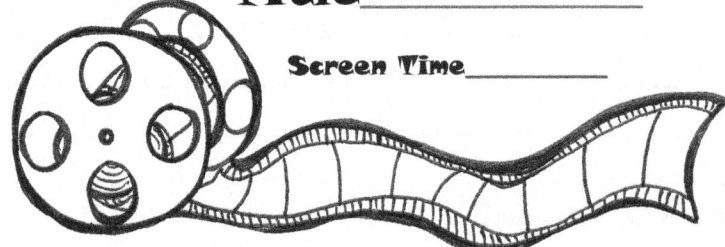

Screen Time_____

Producer_____

Actors_____
_____
_____
_____

Draw it

Pause the video and draw your favorite scene from the film.

Worst

Bad

Awful

Ok

Nice

Great

Best

Make a Comic

Based on the video you watched during screen time.

Title_____

Art Challenge

Draw what you're in the mood to eat. And then go make it.

Math & Design Practice

Use this page for math practice, graphic design, pixel art, and creative measurements.

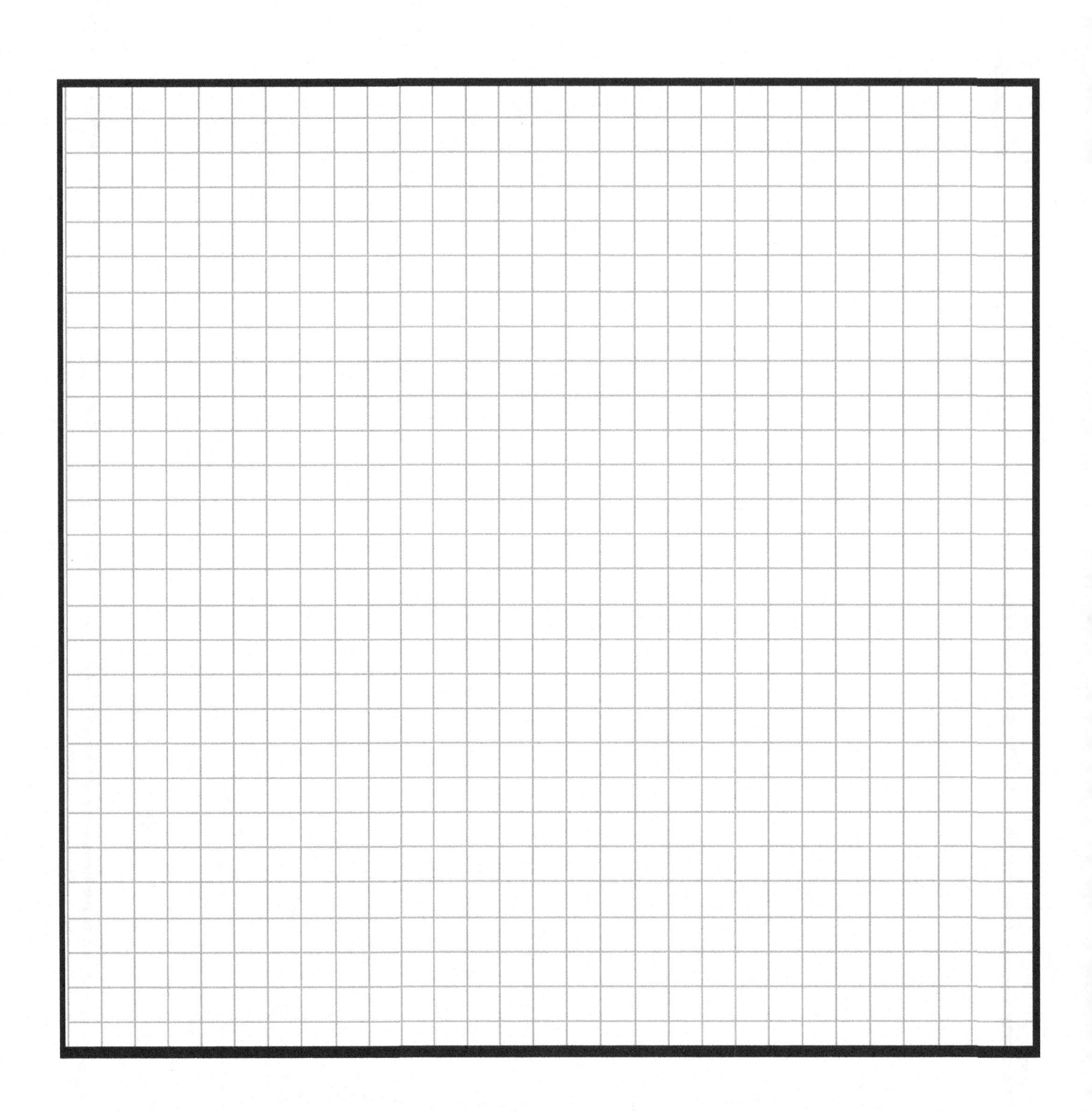

Nature Study

Take this book outside and draw anything and everything that inspires you.

Plans & Priorities

Date: _____

To-do List:
_____
_____
_____
_____
_____

A Quote:
_____
_____
_____
_____

My Goals:
_____
_____
_____
_____
_____

My Plans:
_____
_____
_____
_____

Notes:
_____
_____
_____
_____

Relax & Be Creative

Drawing & Reading Time!

Choose a few books from your stack to focus on today.
Write down and draw what inspires you.
(Set a timer for 1 hour)

Study an Artist
From Ukraine

Name: _____

What is this artist known for?
_____
_____
_____

What makes their artwork unique?
_____
_____
_____
_____
_____

Random fact about this artist or their art:
_____
_____

Write a short biography about this artist:
_____
_____
_____
_____
_____
_____
_____
_____
_____
_____
_____
_____

Design a postage stamp to commemorate this person

Screen Time

Watch a high-quality film, video, tutorial or documentary.

Title_____

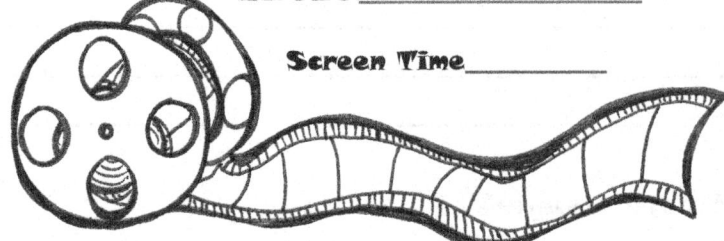

Screen Time_____

Producer_____
Actors_____
_____
_____
_____

Draw it

Pause the video and draw your favorite scene from the film.

Worst

Bad

Awful

Ok

Nice

Great

Best

Make a Comic

Based on the video you watched during screen time.

Title_____

Art Challenge

Draw a beautiful place.
On the next page, draw the same place dirty and polluted.

Math & Design Practice

Use this page for math practice, graphic design, pixel art, and creative measurements.

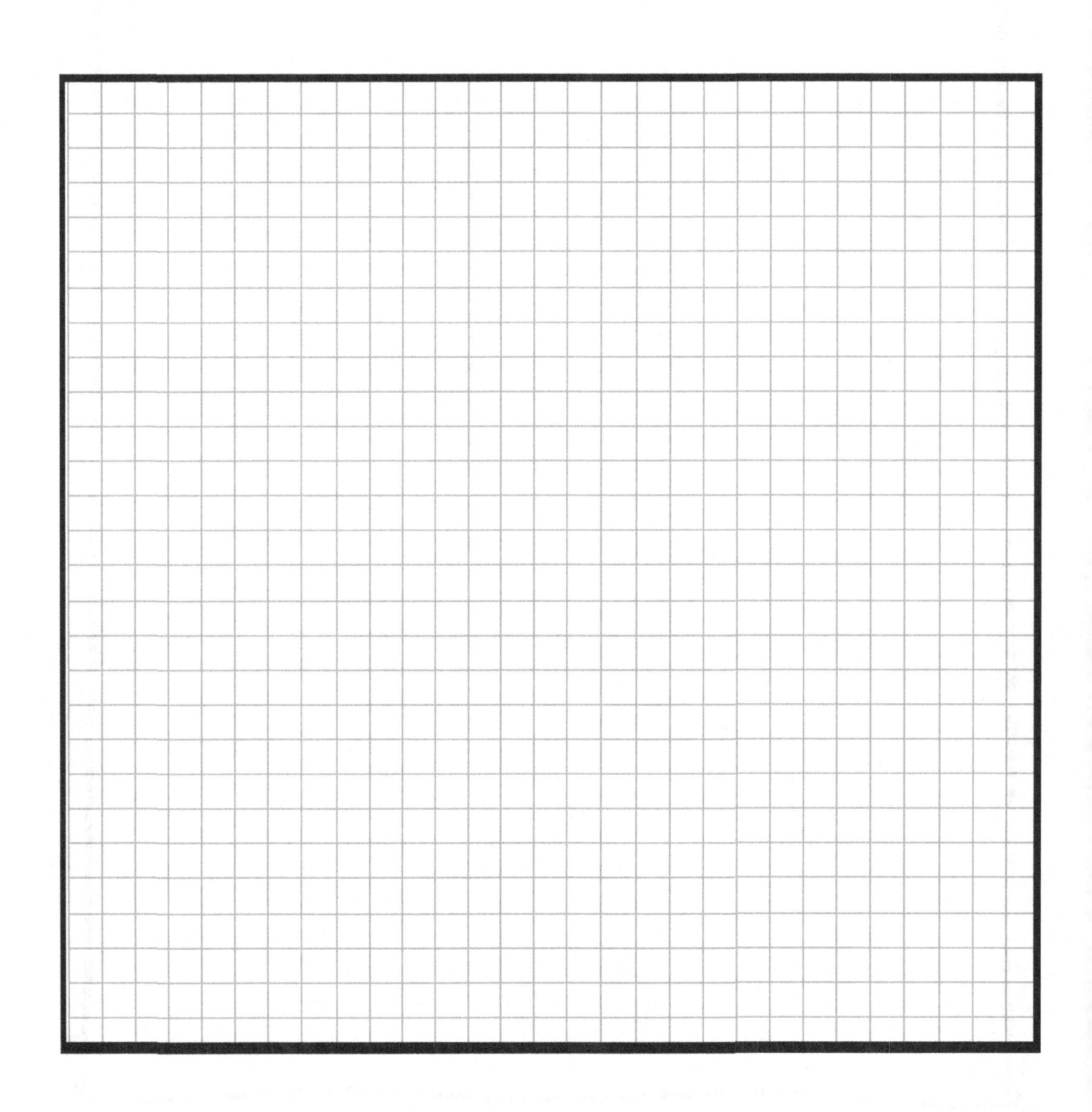

Nature Study

Take this book outside and draw anything and everything that inspires you.

Plans & Priorities

Date: _____

To-do List:
_____
_____
_____
_____
_____

A Quote:
_____
_____
_____
_____

My Goals:
_____
_____
_____
_____

My Plans:
_____
_____
_____
_____

Notes:
_____
_____
_____
_____

Relax & Be Creative

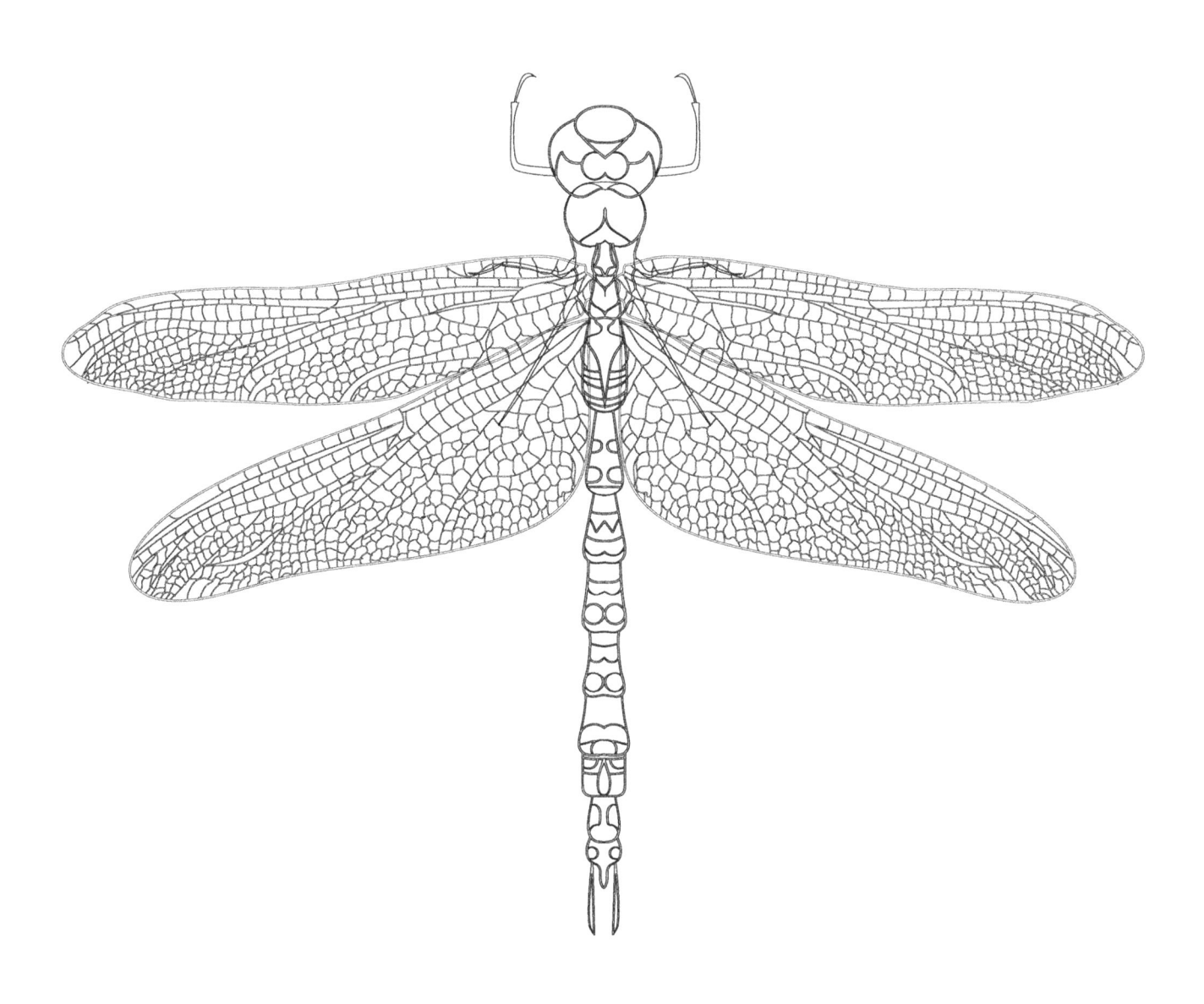

Drawing & Reading Time!

Choose a few books from your stack to focus on today.
Write down and draw what inspires you.
(Set a timer for 1 hour)

Study an Artist
From Russia

Name:_____

What is this artist known for?
_____
_____
_____

What makes their artwork unique?
_____
_____
_____
_____
_____

Random fact about this artist or their art:
_____
_____

Write a short biography about this artist:
_____
_____
_____
_____
_____
_____
_____
_____
_____
_____
_____
_____

Design a postage stamp to commemorate this person

Screen Time

Watch a high-quality film, video, tutorial or documentary.

Title_____

Screen Time_____

Producer_____

Actors_____

_____

_____

_____

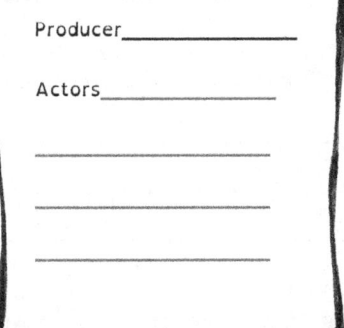

Draw it

Pause the video and draw your favorite scene from the film.

Worst

Bad

Awful

Ok

Nice

Great

Best

Make a Comic

Based on the video you watched during screen time.

Title_____

Art Challenge

Draw rags to riches: Below, draw a rich person.
On the next page, draw the same person very poor.

Math & Design Practice

Use this page for math practice, graphic design, pixel art, and creative measurements.

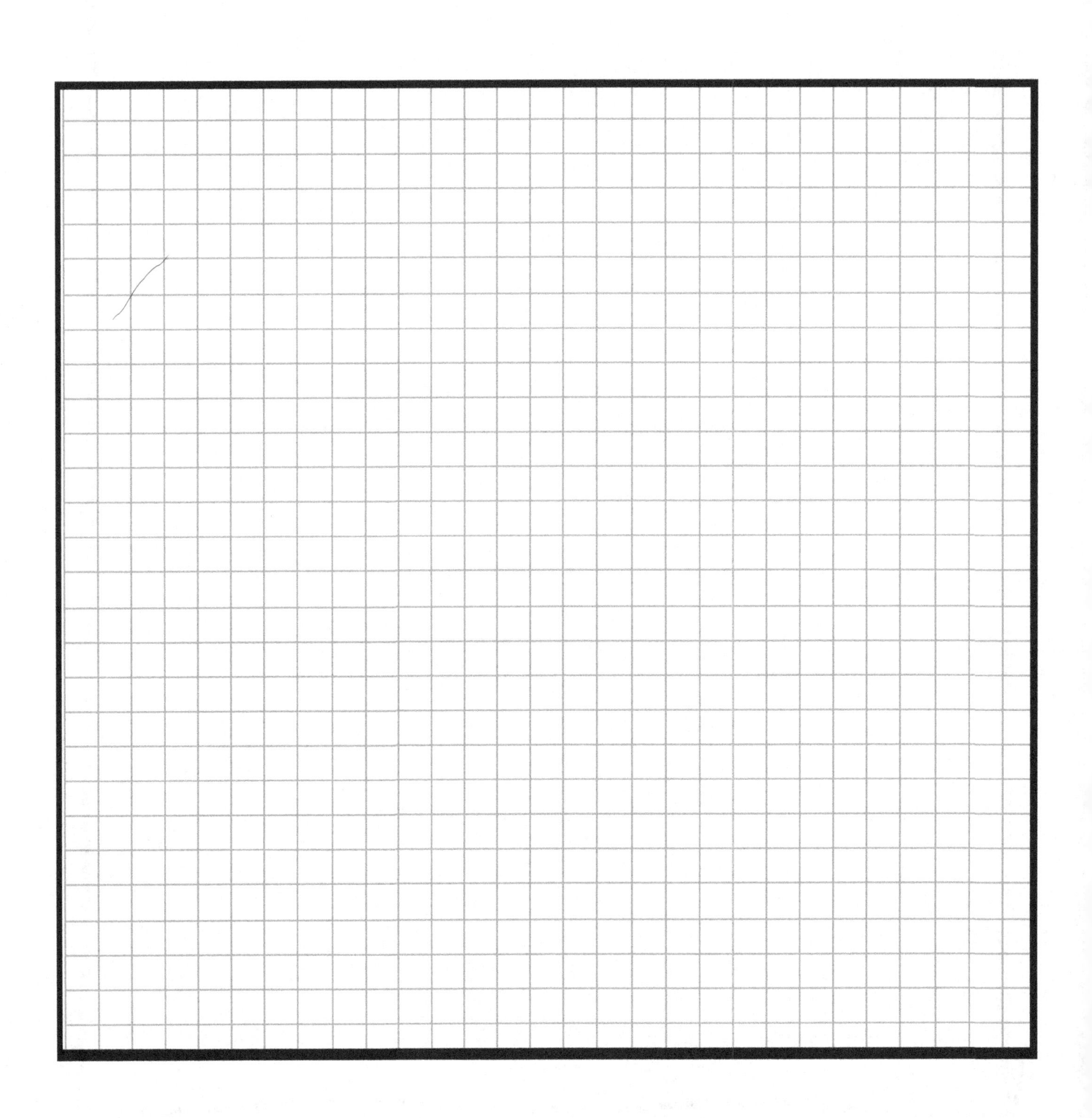

Nature Study

Take this book outside and draw anything and everything that inspires you.

Plans & Priorities

Date:_____

To-do List:
_____
_____
_____
_____
_____

A Quote:
_____
_____
_____
_____
_____

My Goals:
_____
_____
_____
_____
_____

My Plans:
_____
_____
_____
_____
_____

Notes:
_____
_____
_____
_____

Relax & Be Creative

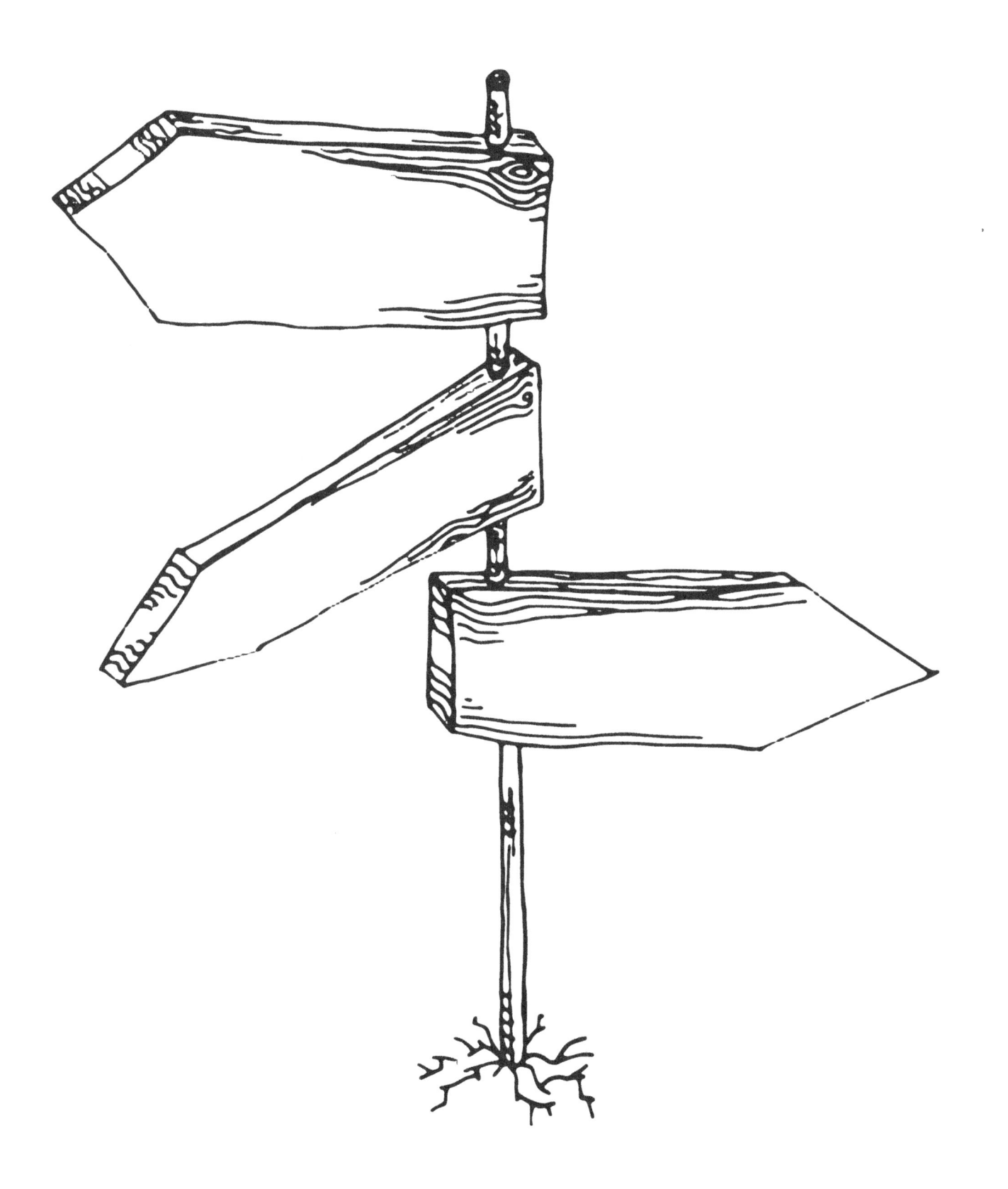

Drawing & Reading Time!

Choose a few books from your stack to focus on today.
Write down and draw what inspires you.
(Set a timer for 1 hour)

Study an Artist
You choose!

Name: _____

What is this artist known for?
_____
_____
_____

What makes their artwork unique?
_____
_____
_____
_____
_____

Random fact about this artist or their art:
_____
_____

Write a short biography about this artist:
_____
_____
_____
_____
_____
_____
_____
_____
_____
_____
_____
_____

Design a postage stamp to commemorate this person

Screen Time

Watch a high-quality film, video, tutorial or documentary.

Title_____

Screen Time_____

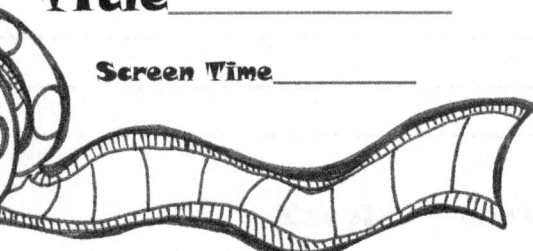

Producer_____

Actors_____

_____

_____

_____

Draw it

Pause the video and draw your favorite scene from the film.

Worst

Bad

Awful

Ok

Nice

Great

Best

Make a Comic

Based on the video you watched during screen time.

Title_____

Art Challenge

Draw a scene from the Bible.

Math & Design Practice

Use this page for math practice, graphic design, pixel art, and creative measurements.

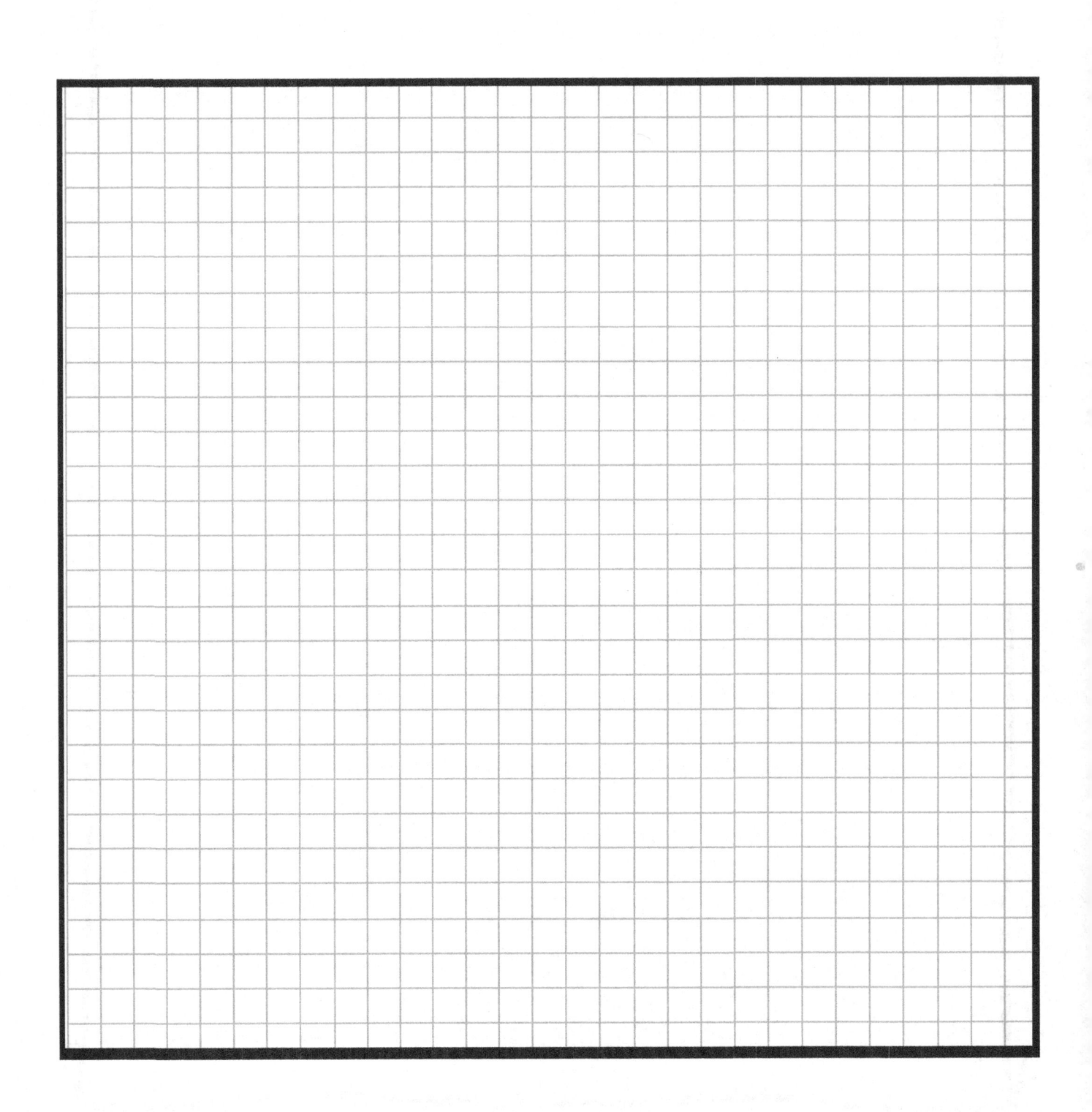

Nature Study

Take this book outside and draw anything and everything that inspires you.

Plans & Priorities

Date:_____

To-do List:
_____
_____
_____
_____
_____

A Quote:
_____
_____
_____
_____
_____

My Goals:
_____
_____
_____
_____

My Plans:
_____
_____
_____
_____
_____

Notes:
_____
_____
_____
_____

Relax & Be Creative

Drawing & Reading Time!

Choose a few books from your stack to focus on today.
Write down and draw what inspires you.
(Set a timer for 1 hour)

Study an Artist
From Africa

Name:_____

What is this artist known for?
_____
_____
_____

What makes their artwork unique?
_____
_____
_____
_____
_____

Random fact about this artist or their art:
_____
_____

Write a short biography about this artist:
_____
_____
_____
_____
_____
_____
_____
_____
_____
_____
_____
_____

Design a postage stamp to commemorate this person

Screen Time

Watch a high-quality film, video, tutorial or documentary.

Title_____

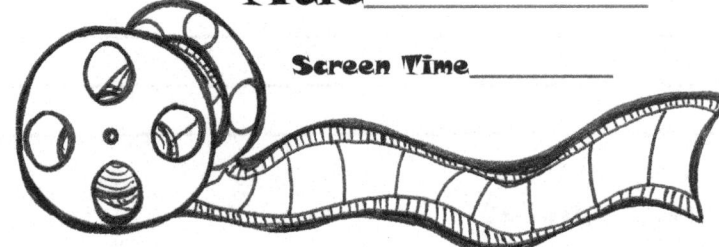

Screen Time_____

Producer_____
Actors_____
_____
_____
_____
_____

Draw it

Pause the video and draw your favorite scene from the film.

Worst

Bad

Awful

Ok

Nice

Great

Best

Make a Comic

Based on the video you watched during screen time.

Title_____

Art Challenge

Go somewhere peaceful and put on headphones.
Play a playlist on shuffle and draw a picture
inspired by the first song that plays.

Math & Design Practice

Use this page for math practice, graphic design, pixel art, and creative measurements.

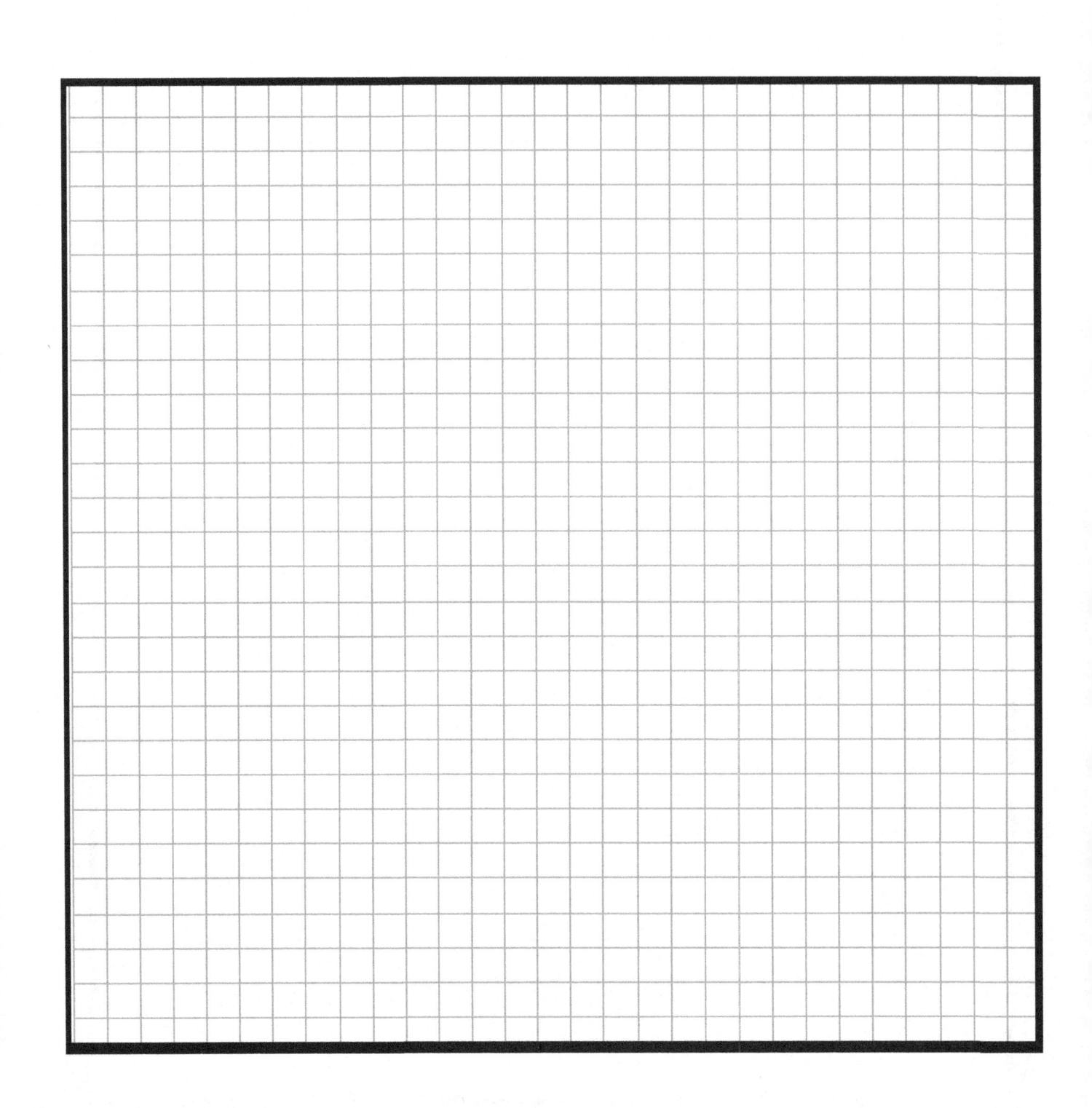

Nature Study

Take this book outside and draw anything and everything that inspires you.

Plans & Priorities

Date: _____

To-do List:
_____
_____
_____
_____
_____

A Quote:
_____
_____
_____
_____

My Goals:
_____
_____
_____
_____
_____

My Plans:
_____
_____
_____
_____

Notes:
_____
_____
_____
_____

Relax & Be Creative

Drawing & Reading Time!

Choose a few books from your stack to focus on today.
Write down and draw what inspires you.
(Set a timer for 1 hour)

Study an Artist
From the 1700's

Name: _____

What is this artist known for?
_____
_____
_____

What makes their artwork unique?
_____
_____
_____
_____
_____

Random fact about this artist or their art:
_____
_____

Write a short biography about this artist:
_____
_____
_____
_____
_____
_____
_____
_____
_____
_____
_____
_____

Design a postage stamp to commemorate this person

Screen Time

Watch a high-quality film, video, tutorial or documentary.

Title_____

Screen Time_____

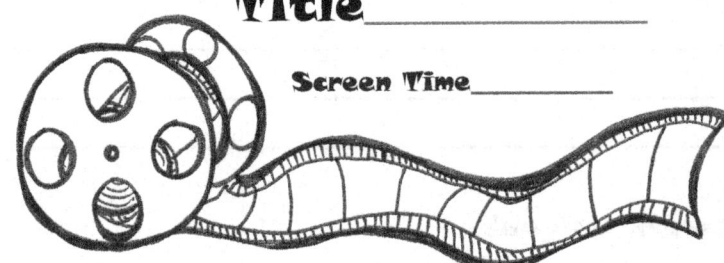

Producer_____

Actors_____
_____
_____
_____

Draw it

Pause the video and draw your favorite scene from the film.

Worst

Bad

Awful

Ok

Nice

Great

Best

Make a Comic

Based on the video you watched during screen time.

Title_____

Art Challenge

Draw yourself conquering your greatest fear.

Math & Design Practice

Use this page for math practice, graphic design, pixel art, and creative measurements.

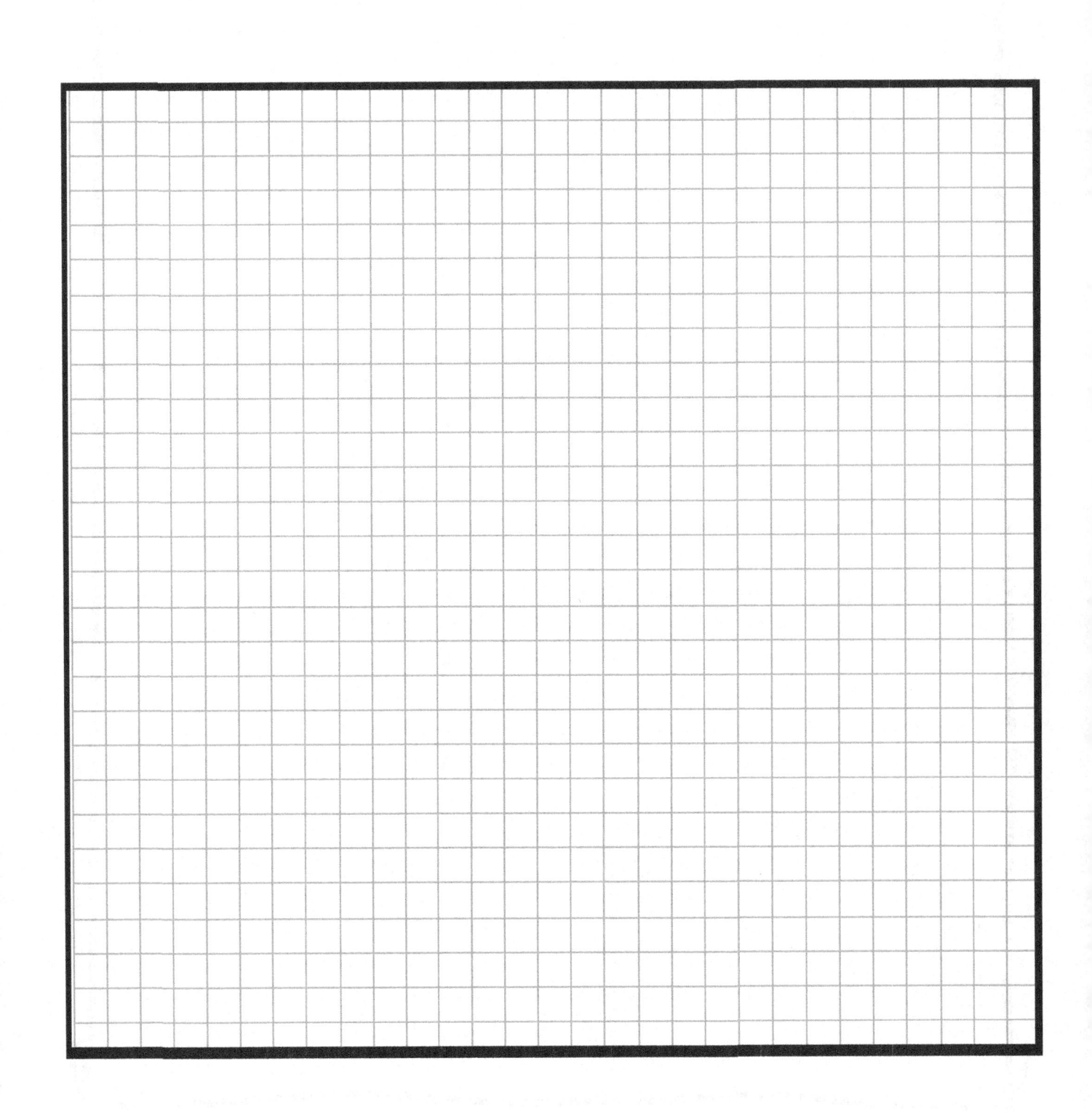

Nature Study

Take this book outside and draw anything and everything that inspires you.

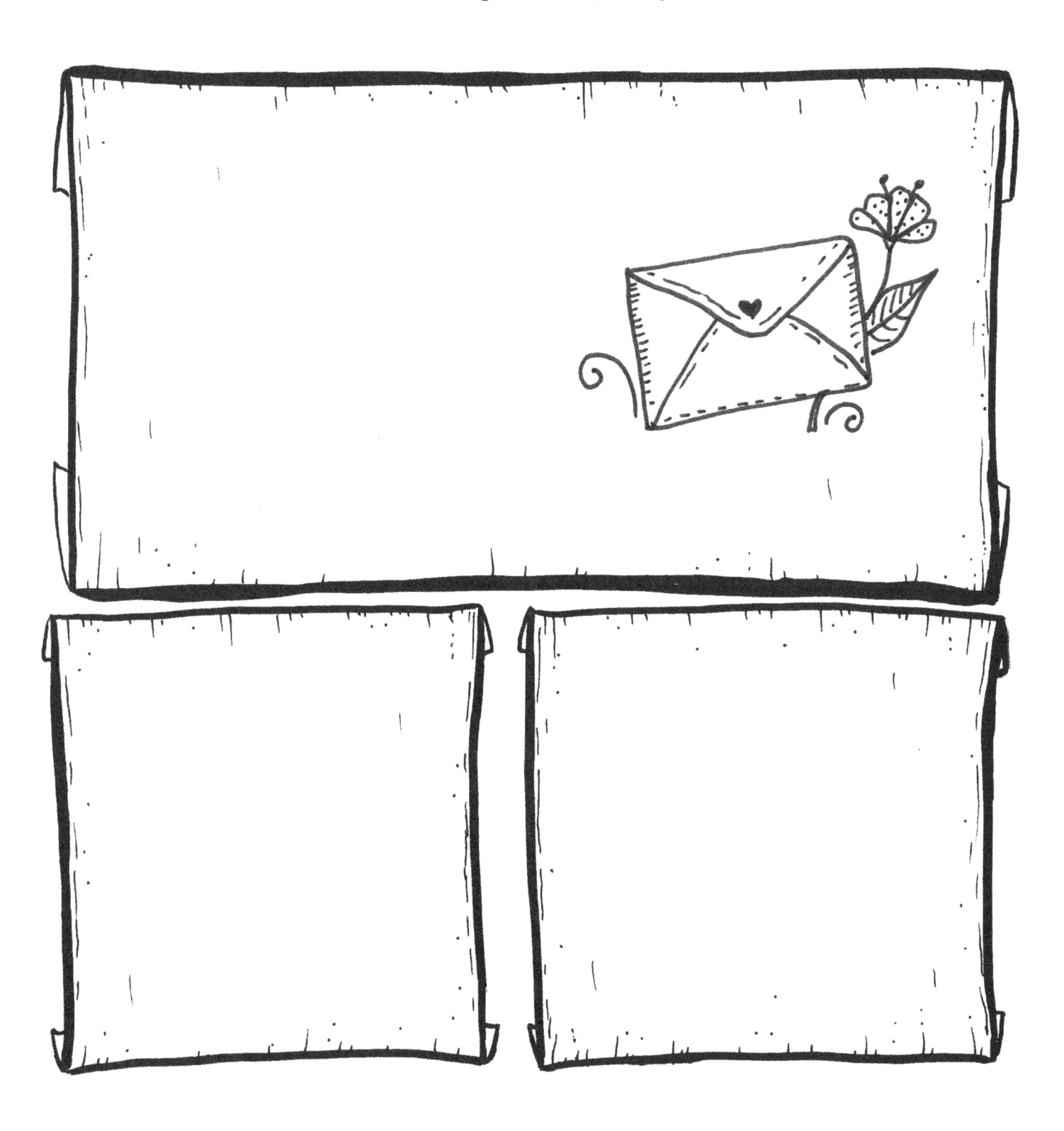

Plans & Priorities

Date:_____

To-do List:
_____
_____
_____
_____
_____

A Quote:
_____
_____
_____
_____
_____

My Goals:
_____
_____
_____
_____
_____

My Plans:
_____
_____
_____
_____
_____

Notes:
_____
_____
_____
_____

Relax & Be Creative

Drawing & Reading Time!

Choose a few books from your stack to focus on today.
Write down and draw what inspires you.
(Set a timer for 1 hour)

Study an Artist
From South America

Name: _____

What is this artist known for?
_____
_____
_____

What makes their artwork unique?
_____
_____
_____
_____
_____

Random fact about this artist or their art:
_____
_____

Write a short biography about this artist:
_____
_____
_____
_____
_____
_____
_____
_____
_____
_____
_____
_____

Design a postage stamp to commemorate this person

Screen Time

Watch a high-quality film, video, tutorial or documentary.

Title_____

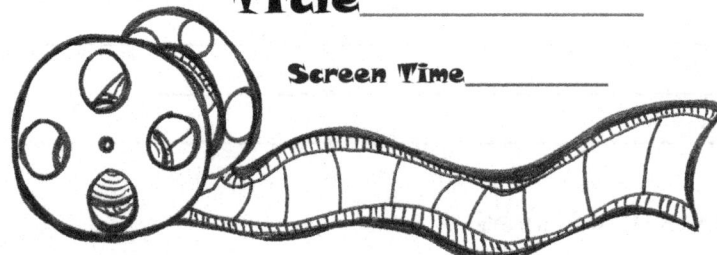

Screen Time_____

Producer_____

Actors_____
_____
_____
_____

Draw it

Pause the video and draw your favorite scene from the film.

Worst

Bad

Awful

Ok

Nice

Great

Best

Make a Comic

Based on the video you watched during screen time.

Title_____

Art Challenge

Draw a scene from your favorite movie.

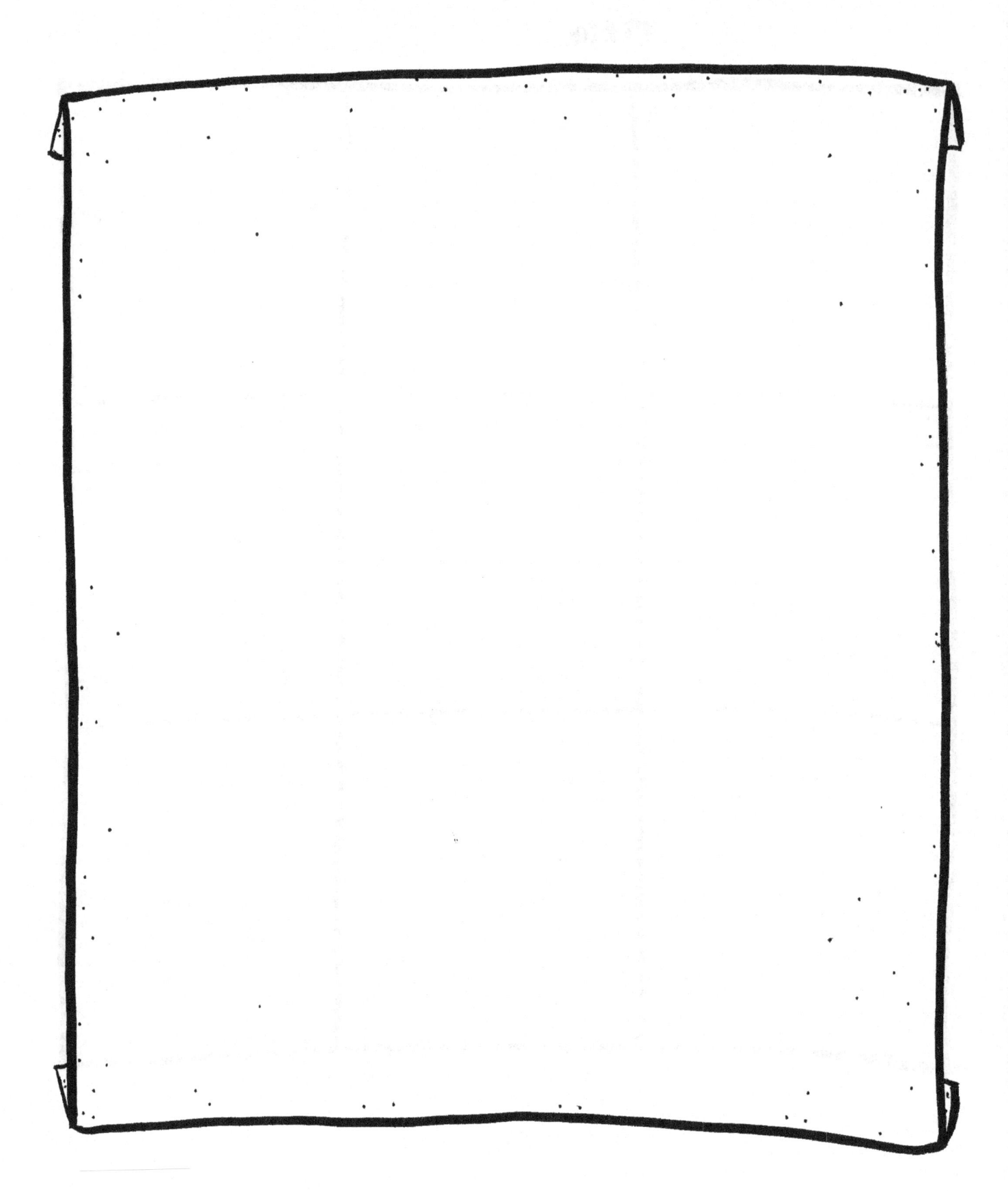

Math & Design Practice

Use this page for math practice, graphic design, pixel art, and creative measurements.

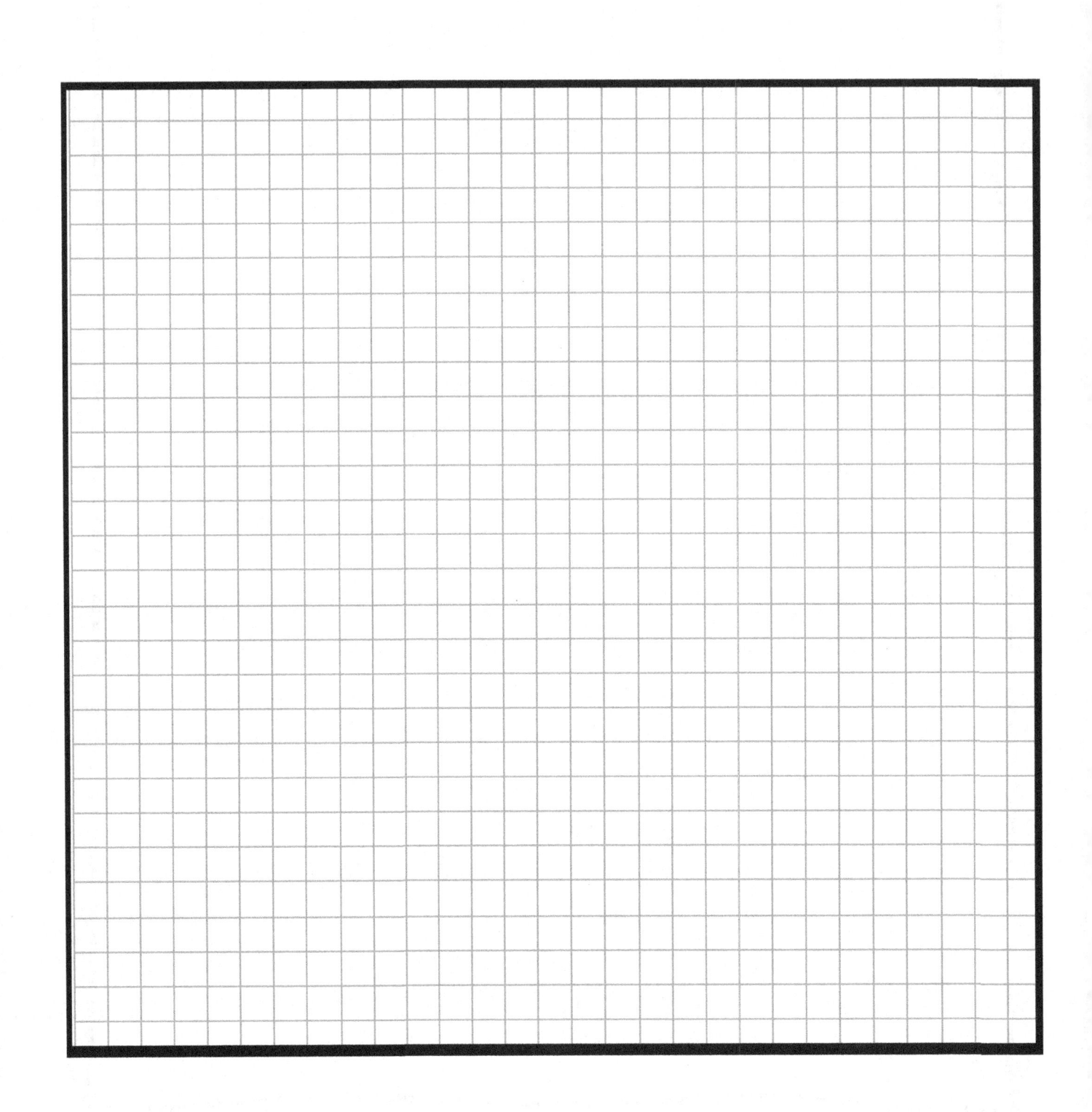

Nature Study

Take this book outside and draw anything and everything that inspires you.

Plans & Priorities

Date: _____

To-do List:
_____
_____
_____
_____
_____

A Quote:
_____
_____
_____
_____
_____

My Goals:
_____
_____
_____
_____
_____

My Plans:
_____
_____
_____
_____
_____

Notes:
_____
_____
_____
_____

Relax & Be Creative

Drawing & Reading Time!

Choose a few books from your stack to focus on today.
Write down and draw what inspires you.
(Set a timer for 1 hour)

Study an Artist
From Canada

Name:_____

What is this artist known for?
_____
_____
_____

What makes their artwork unique?
_____
_____
_____
_____
_____
_____

Random fact about this artist or their art:
_____
_____

Write a short biography about this artist:
_____
_____
_____
_____
_____
_____
_____
_____
_____
_____
_____
_____

Design a postage stamp to commemorate this person

Art Challenge

Draw in a style you've never tried.

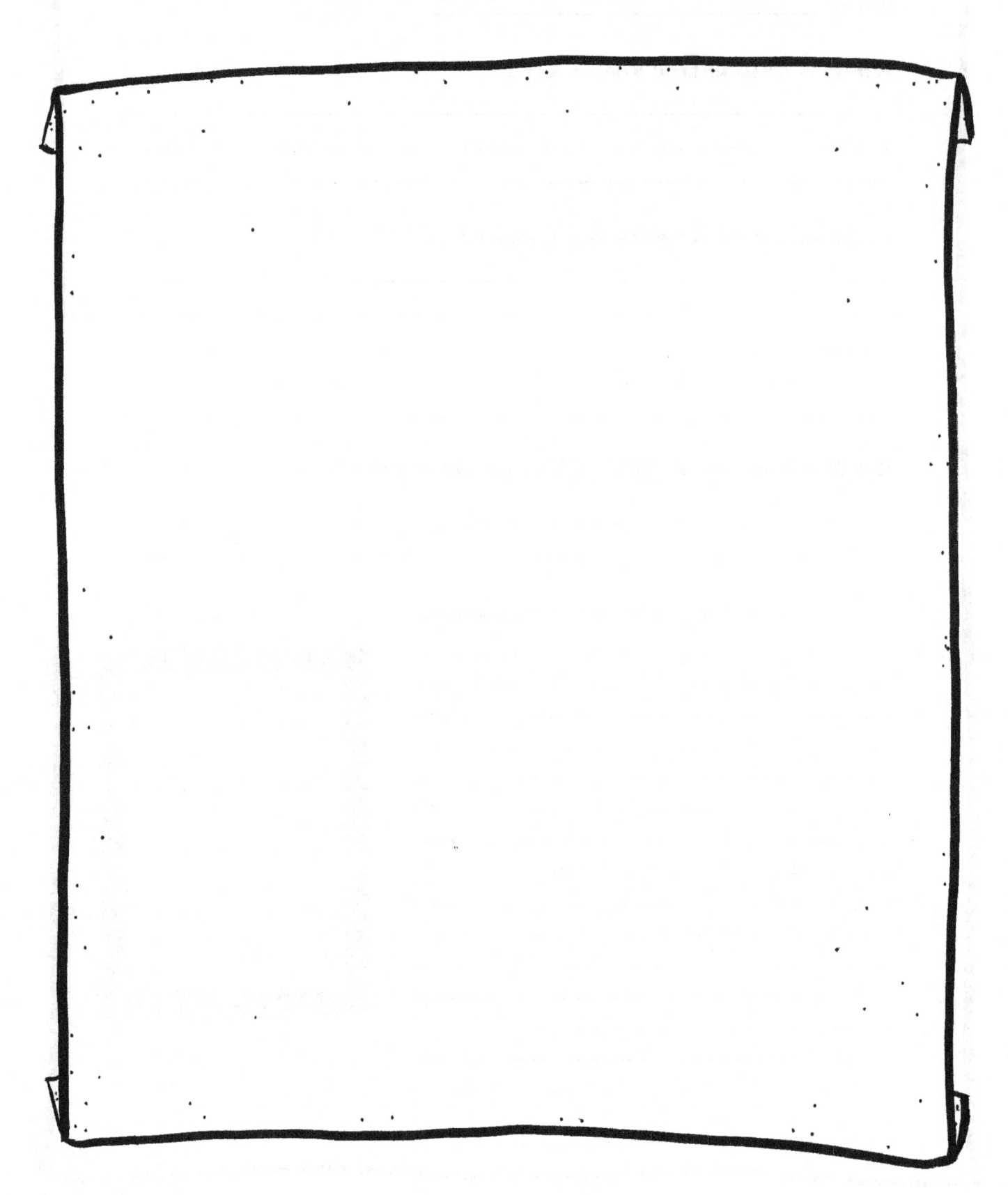

Math & Design Practice

Use this page for math practice, graphic design, pixel art, and creative measurements.

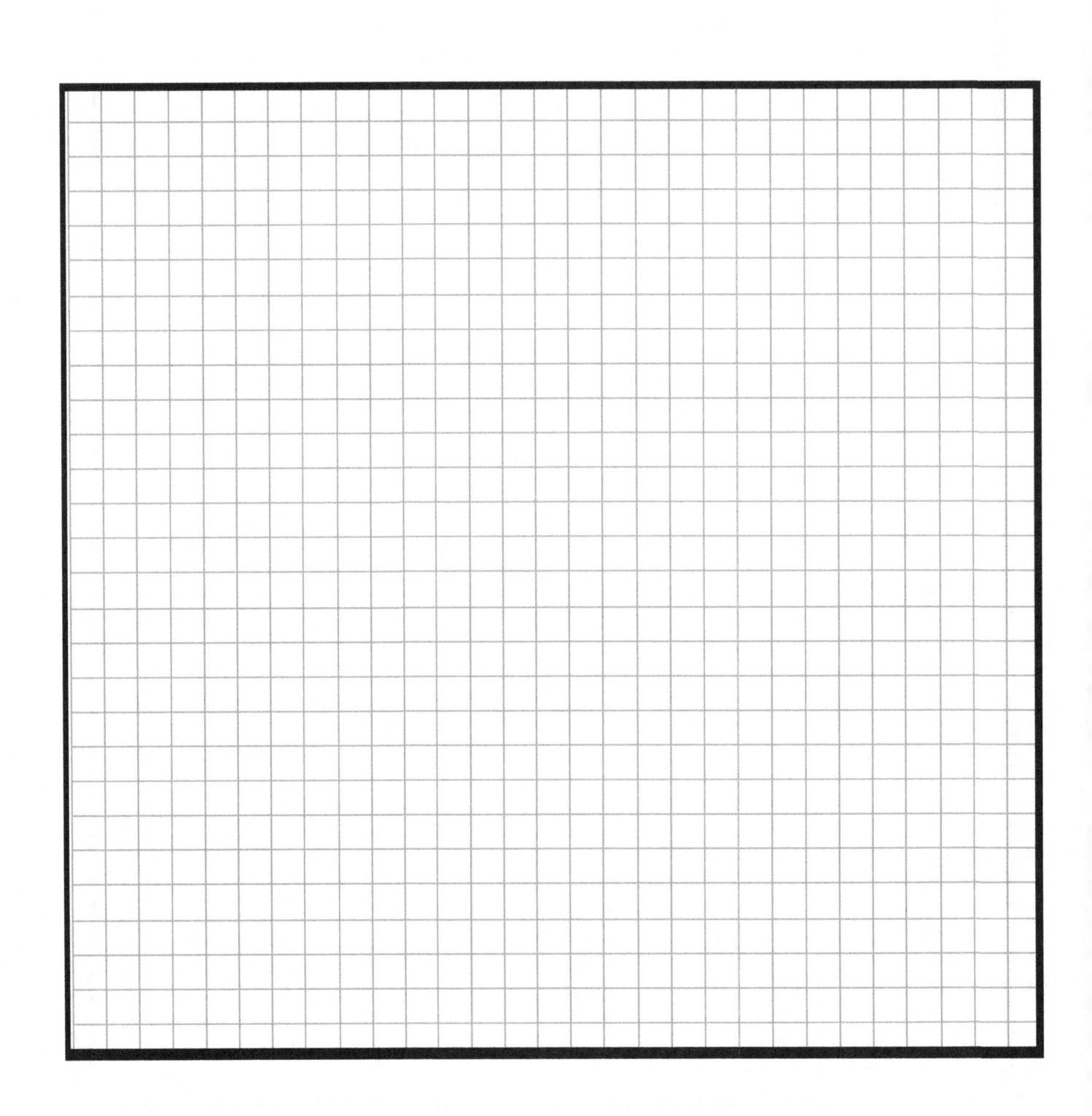

Nature Study

Take this book outside and draw anything and everything that inspires you.

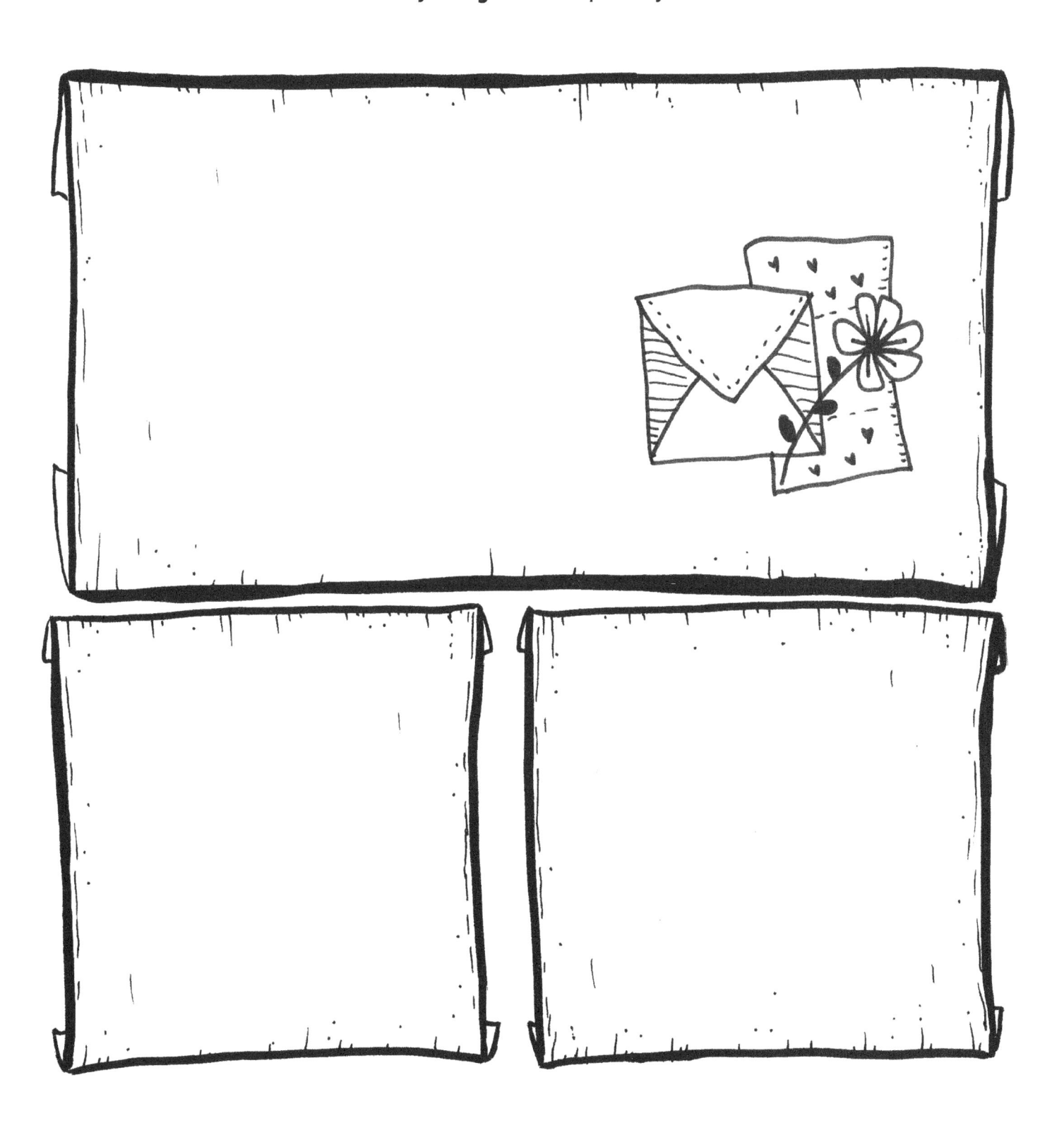

Plans & Priorities

Date: _____

To-do List:
_____
_____
_____
_____

A Quote:
_____
_____
_____
_____

My Goals:
_____
_____
_____
_____

My Plans:
_____
_____
_____
_____

Notes:
_____
_____
_____
_____

Relax & Be Creative

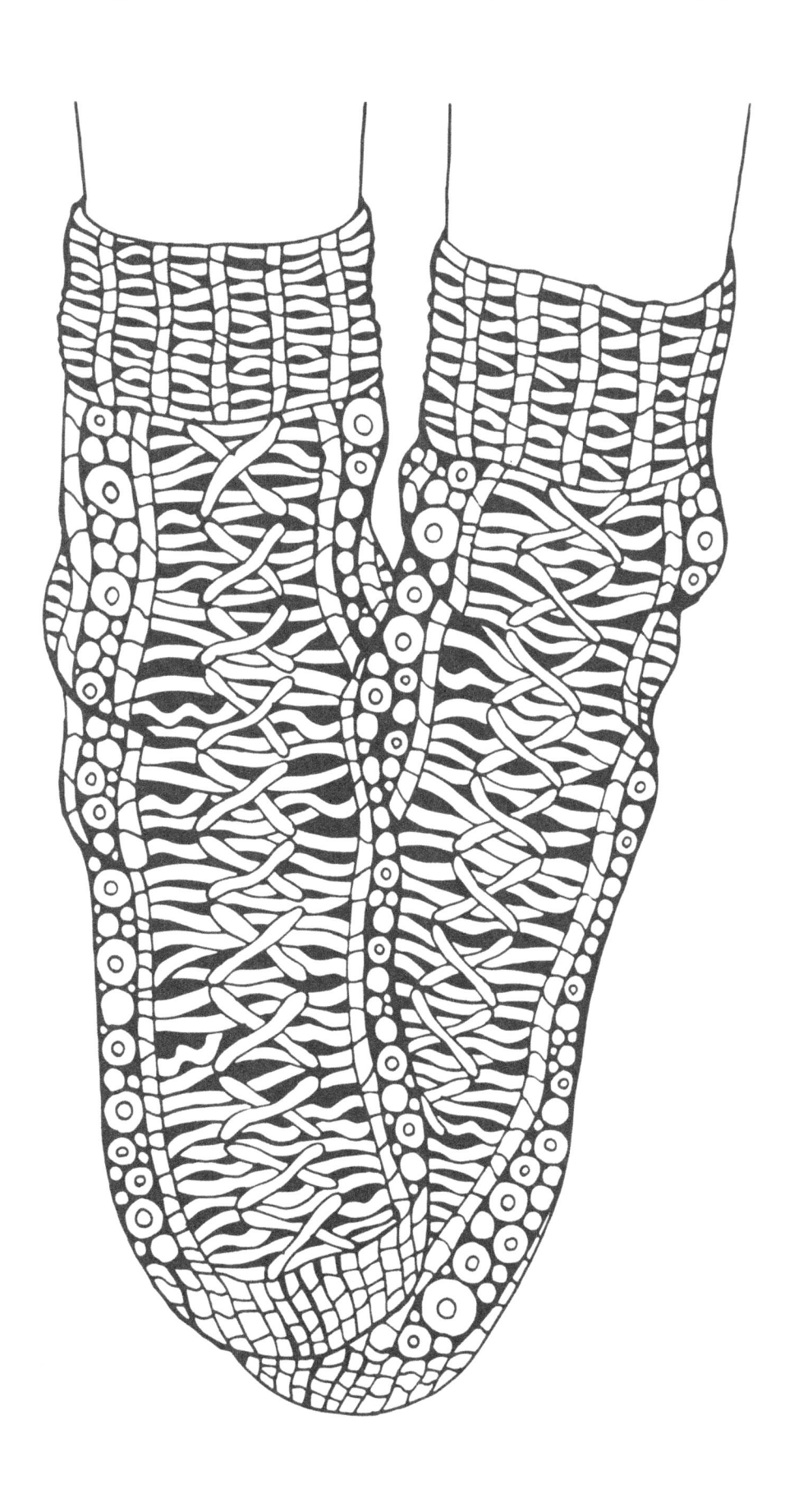

Drawing & Reading Time!

Choose a few books from your stack to focus on today.
Write down and draw what inspires you.
(Set a timer for 1 hour)

Study an Artist
You choose!

Name: _____

What is this artist known for?
_____
_____
_____

What makes their artwork unique?
_____
_____
_____
_____
_____

Random fact about this artist or their art:
_____
_____

Write a short biography about this artist:
_____
_____
_____
_____
_____
_____
_____
_____
_____
_____
_____
_____

Design a postage stamp to commemorate this person

Screen Time

Watch a high-quality film, video, tutorial or documentary.

Title_____

Screen Time_____

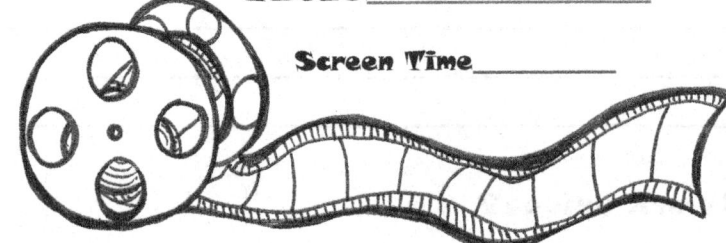

Producer_____

Actors_____
_____
_____
_____

Draw it

Pause the video and draw your favorite scene from the film.

Worst

Bad

Awful

Ok

Nice

Great

Best

Make a Comic

Based on the video you watched during screen time.

Title_____

Art Challenge

Draw a new superhero.

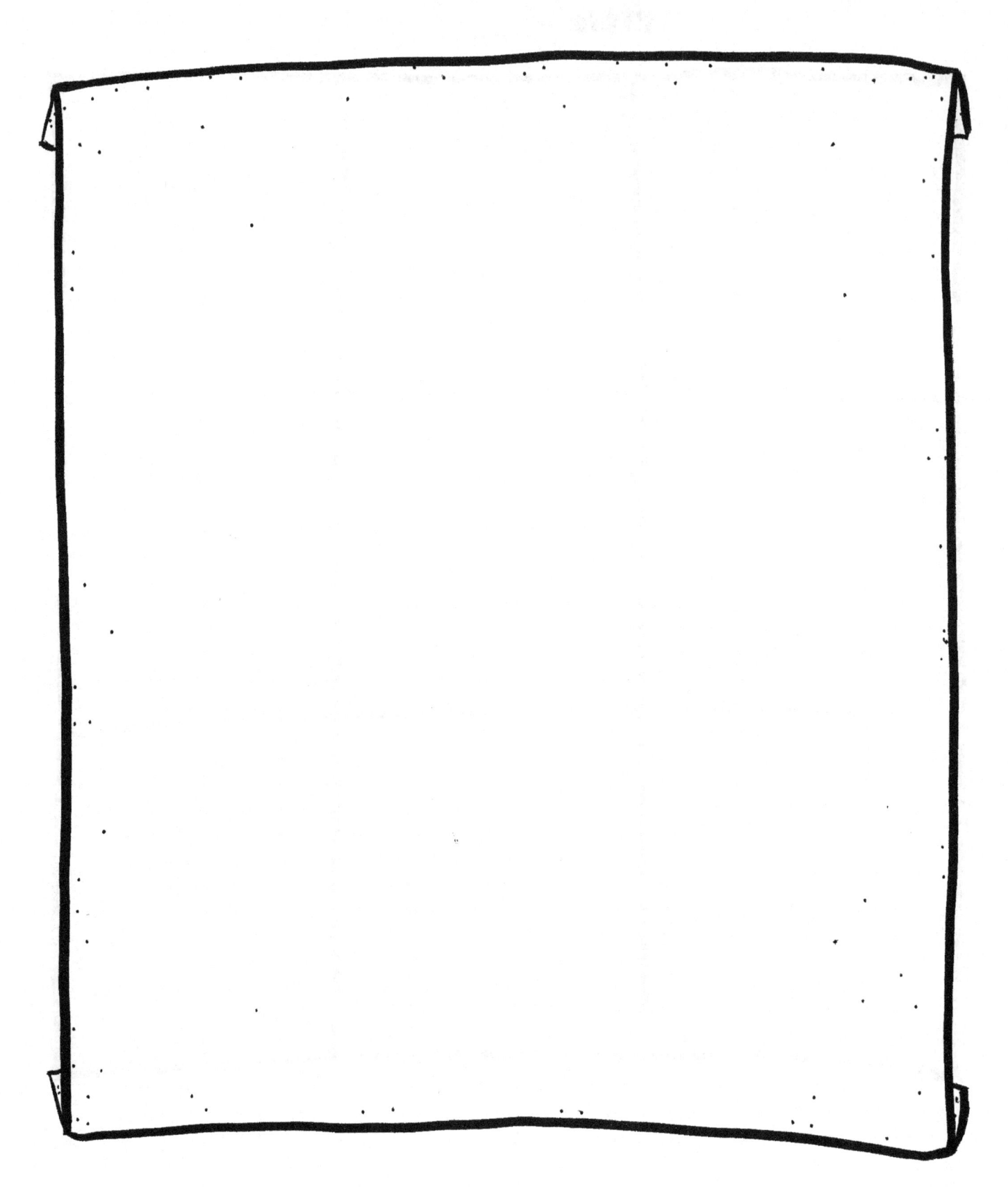

Math & Design Practice

Use this page for math practice, graphic design, pixel art, and creative measurements.

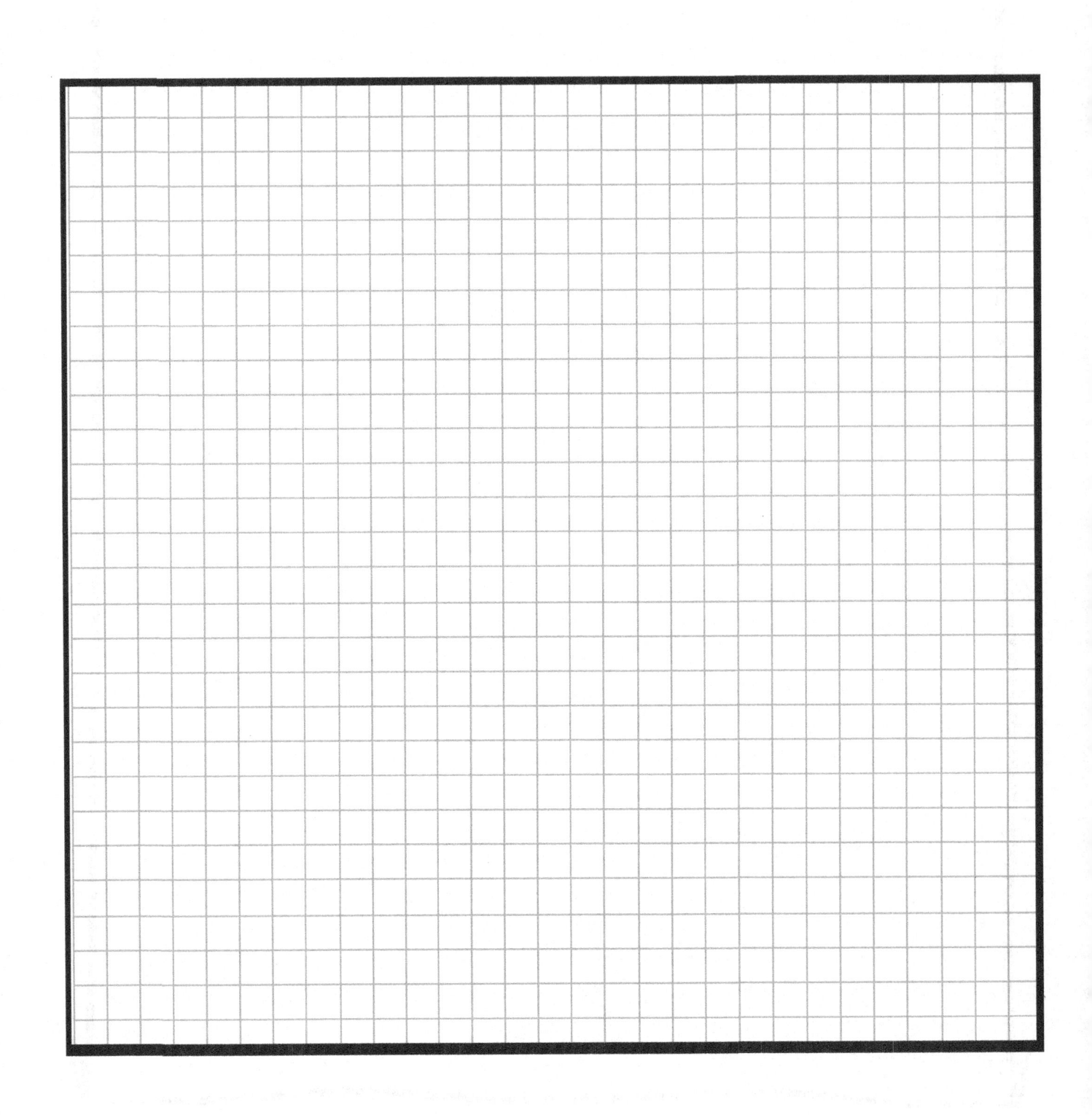

Nature Study

Take this book outside and draw anything and everything that inspires you.

Plans & Priorities

Date:_____

To-do List:
_____
_____
_____
_____
_____

A Quote:
_____
_____
_____
_____
_____

My Goals:
_____
_____
_____
_____
_____

My Plans:
_____
_____
_____
_____
_____

Notes:
_____
_____
_____
_____

Relax & Be Creative

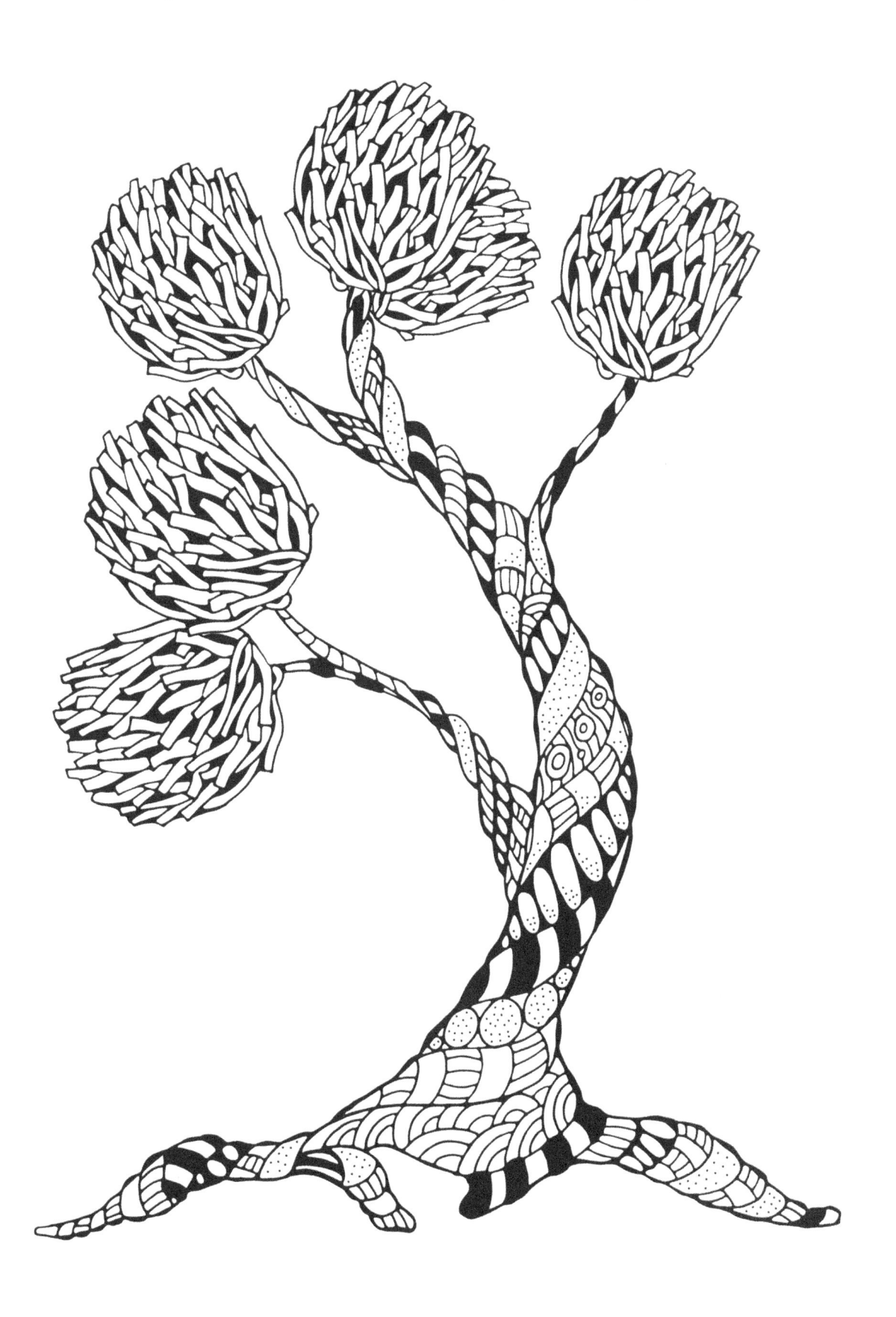

Drawing & Reading Time!

Choose a few books from your stack to focus on today.
Write down and draw what inspires you.
(Set a timer for 1 hour)

Study an Artist
From Spain

Name:_____

What is this artist known for?
_____
_____
_____

What makes their artwork unique?
_____
_____
_____
_____
_____

Random fact about this artist or their art:
_____
_____

Write a short biography about this artist:
_____
_____
_____
_____
_____
_____
_____
_____
_____
_____
_____

Design a postage stamp to commemorate this person

Screen Time

Watch a high-quality film, video, tutorial or documentary.

Title_____

Screen Time_____

Producer_____

Actors_____
_____
_____
_____
_____

Draw it

Pause the video and draw your favorite scene from the film.

Worst

Bad

Awful

Ok

Nice

Great

Best

Make a Comic

Based on the video you watched during screen time.

Title_____

Art Challenge

Draw a cartoon character.

Math & Design Practice

Use this page for math practice, graphic design, pixel art, and creative measurements.

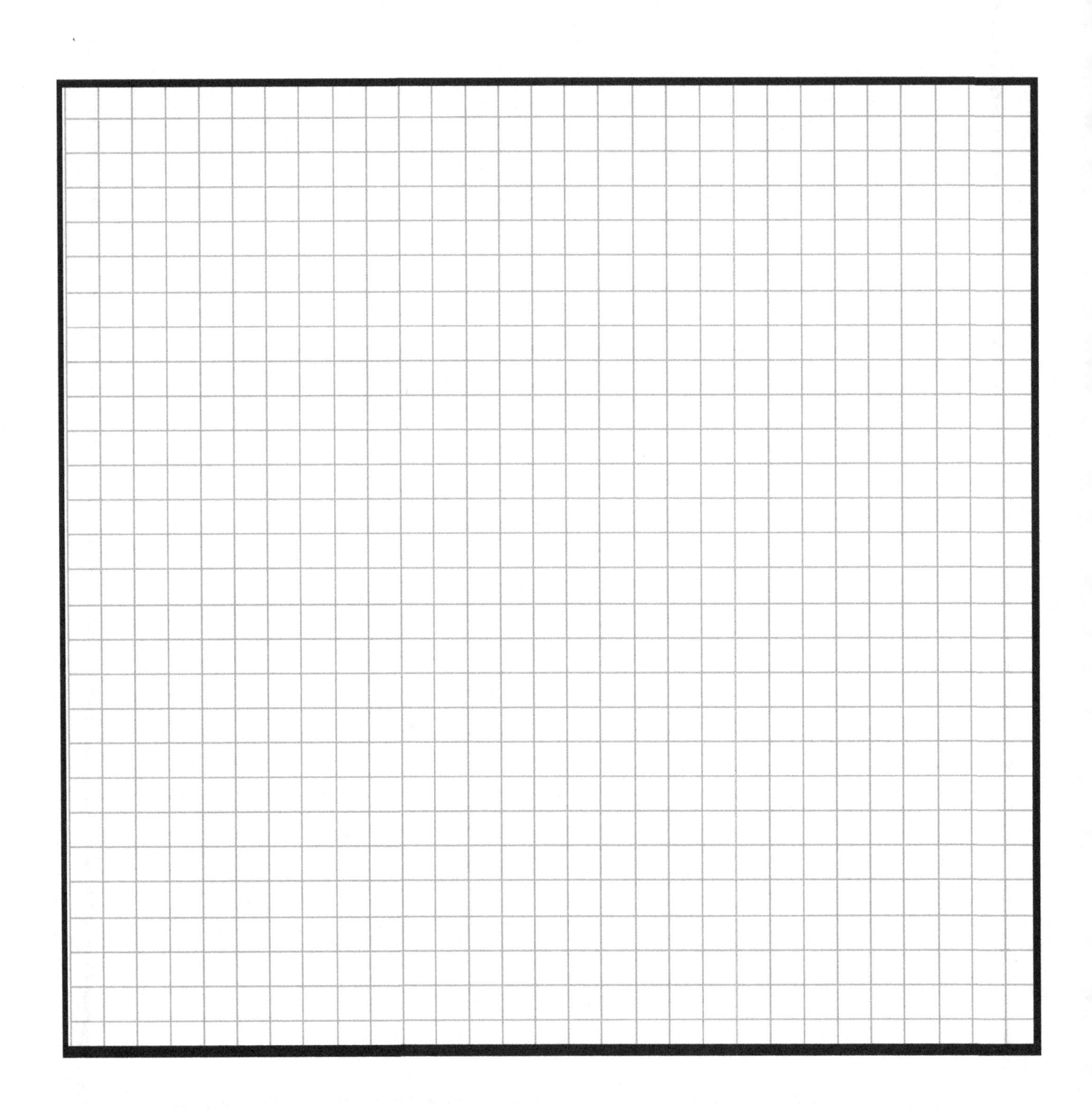

Nature Study

Take this book outside and draw anything and everything that inspires you.

Plans & Priorities

Date: _____

To-do List:
_____
_____
_____
_____

A Quote:
_____
_____
_____
_____

My Goals:
_____
_____
_____
_____

My Plans:
_____
_____
_____
_____

Notes:
_____
_____
_____
_____

Relax & Be Creative

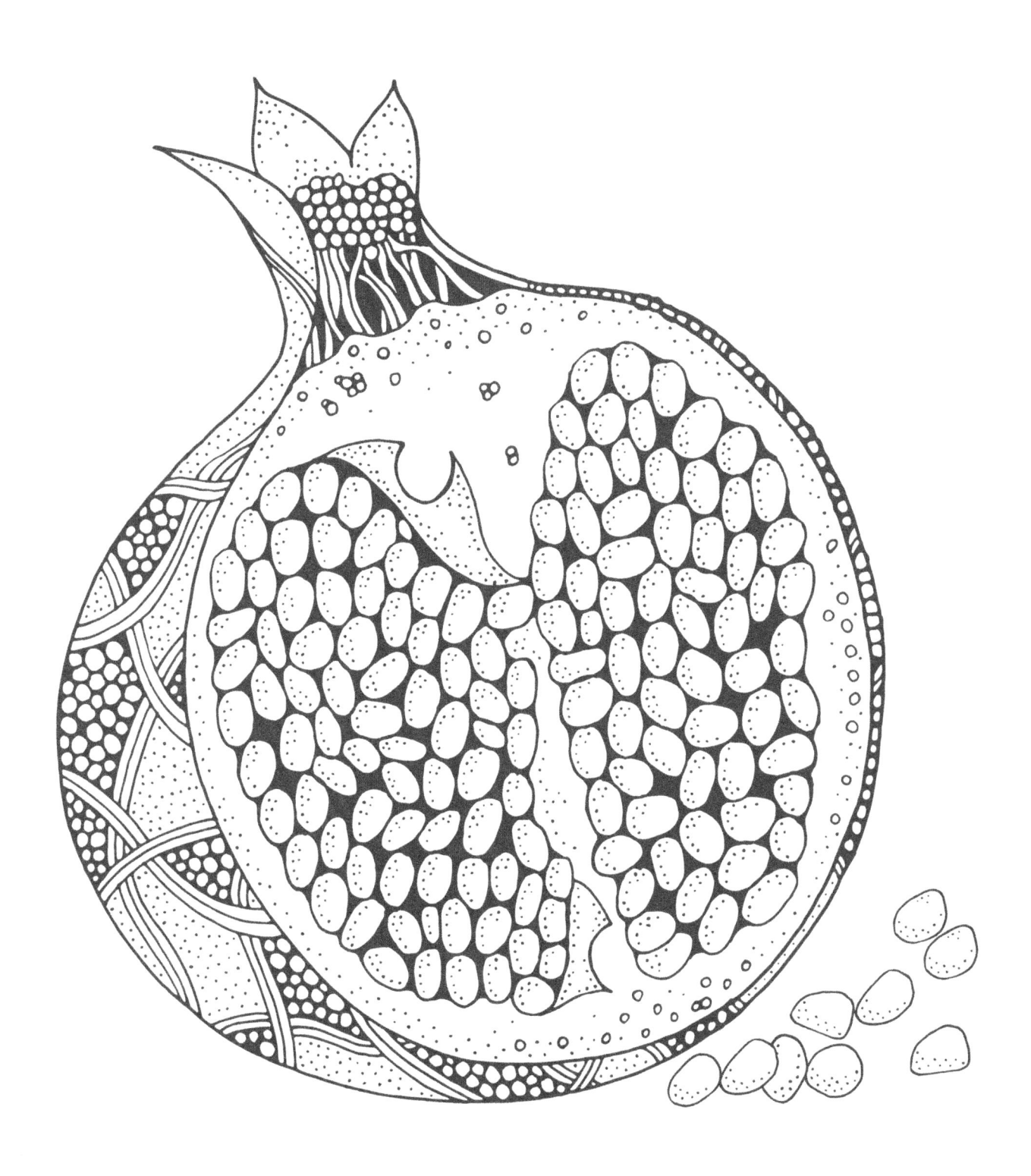

Drawing & Reading Time!

Choose a few books from your stack to focus on today.
Write down and draw what inspires you.
(Set a timer for 1 hour)

Study an Artist
From Mexico

Name: _____

What is this artist known for?
_____
_____
_____

What makes their artwork unique?
_____
_____
_____
_____
_____
_____

Random fact about this artist or their art:
_____
_____

Write a short biography about this artist:
_____
_____
_____
_____
_____
_____
_____
_____
_____
_____
_____
_____
_____
_____

Design a postage stamp to commemorate this person

Screen Time

Watch a high-quality film, video, tutorial or documentary.

Title_____

Screen Time_____

Producer_____

Actors_____
_____
_____
_____

Draw it

Pause the video and draw your favorite scene from the film.

Worst

Bad

Awful

Ok

Nice

Great

Best

Make a Comic

Based on the video you watched during screen time.

Title_____

Art Challenge

Draw yourself doing your dream job.

Math & Design Practice

Use this page for math practice, graphic design, pixel art, and creative measurements.

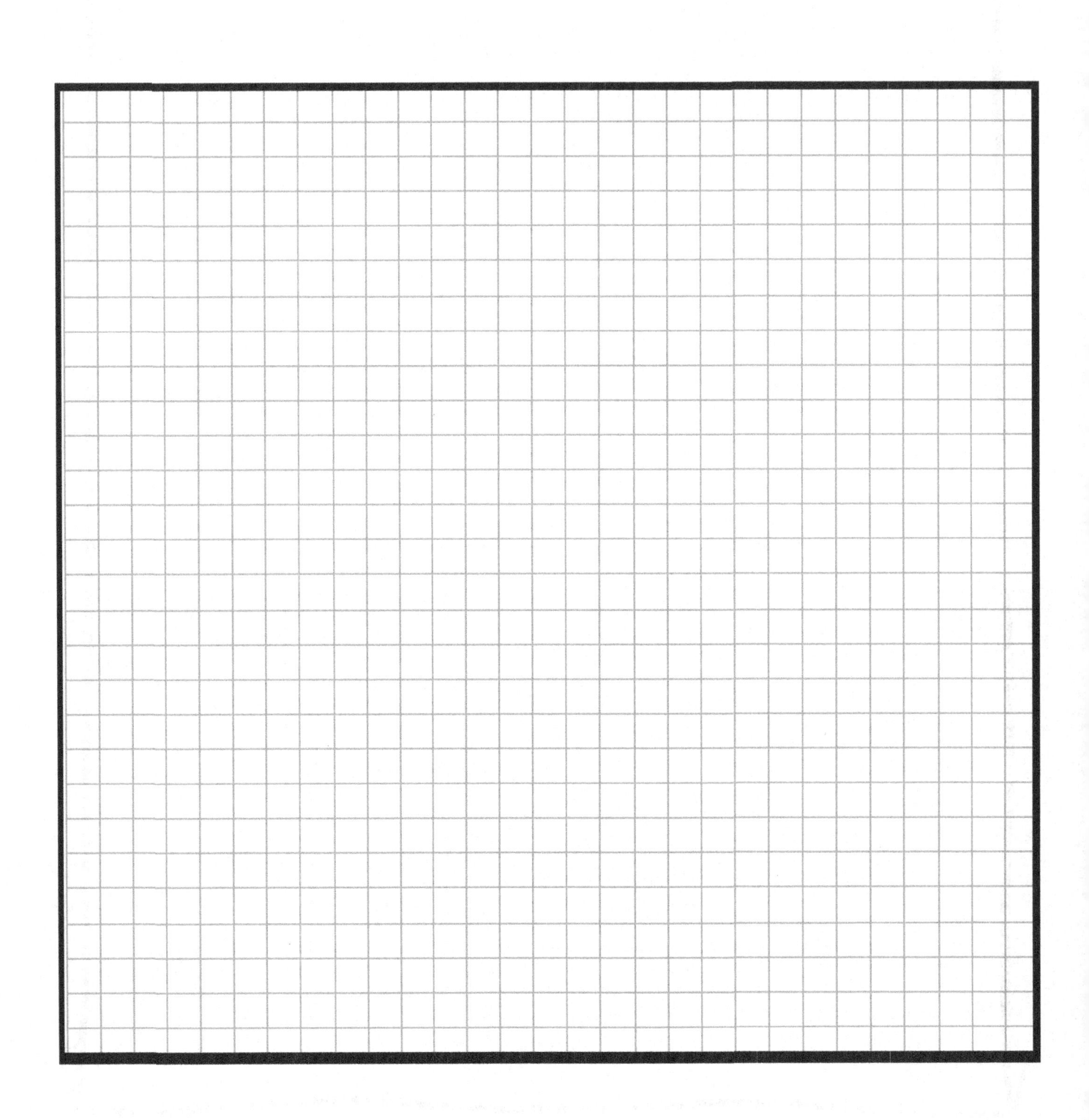

Nature Study

Take this book outside and draw anything and everything that inspires you.

Plans & Priorities

Date:_____

To-do List:
_____
_____
_____
_____

A Quote:
_____
_____
_____
_____

My Goals:
_____
_____
_____
_____

My Plans:
_____
_____
_____
_____

Notes:
_____
_____
_____
_____

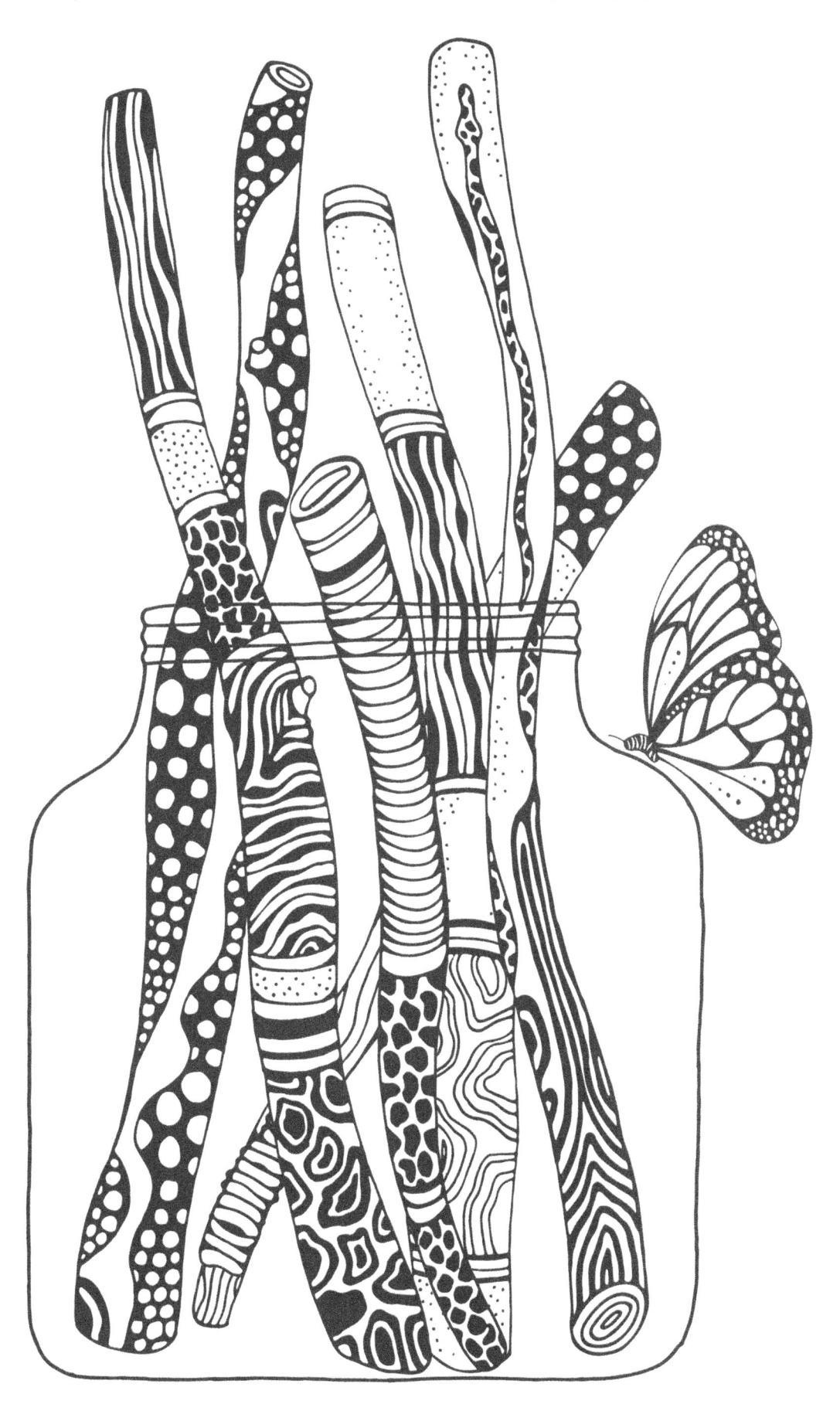

Relax & Be Creative

Drawing & Reading Time!

Choose a few books from your stack to focus on today.
Write down and draw what inspires you.
(Set a timer for 1 hour)

Study an Artist
From the 1800's

Name:_____

What is this artist known for?
_____
_____
_____

What makes their artwork unique?
_____
_____
_____
_____
_____

Random fact about this artist or their art:
_____
_____

Write a short biography about this artist:
_____
_____
_____
_____
_____
_____
_____
_____
_____
_____
_____

Design a postage stamp to commemorate this person

Screen Time

Watch a high-quality film, video, tutorial or documentary.

Title_____

Screen Time_____

Producer_____

Actors_____
_____
_____
_____

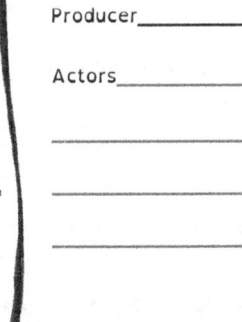

Draw it

Pause the video and draw your favorite scene from the film.

Worst

Bad

Awful

Ok

Nice

Great

Best

Make a Comic

Based on the video you watched during screen time.

Title_____

Art Challenge

Draw something terrifying.

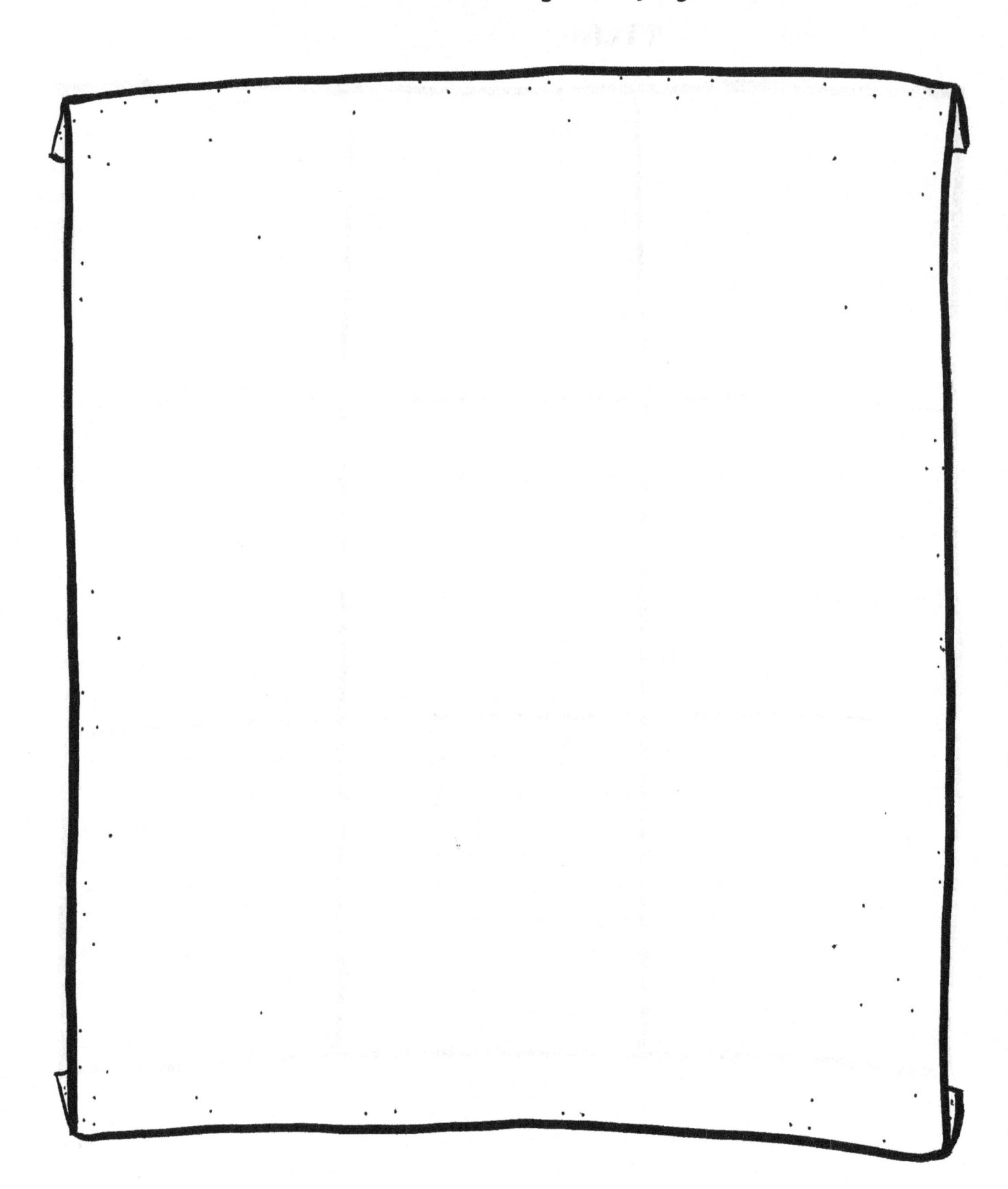

Math & Design Practice

Use this page for math practice, graphic design, pixel art, and creative measurements.

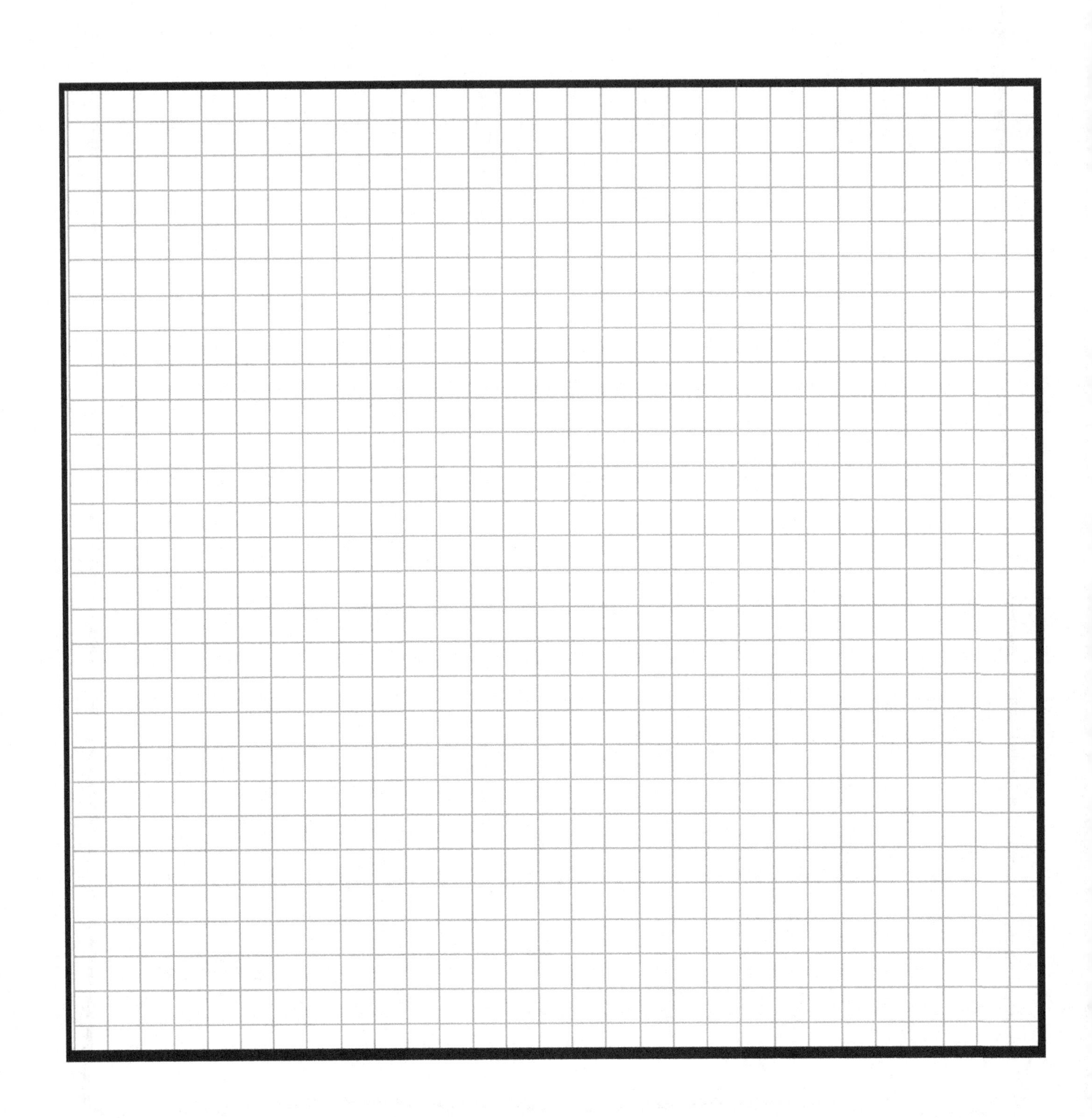

Nature Study

Take this book outside and draw anything and everything that inspires you.

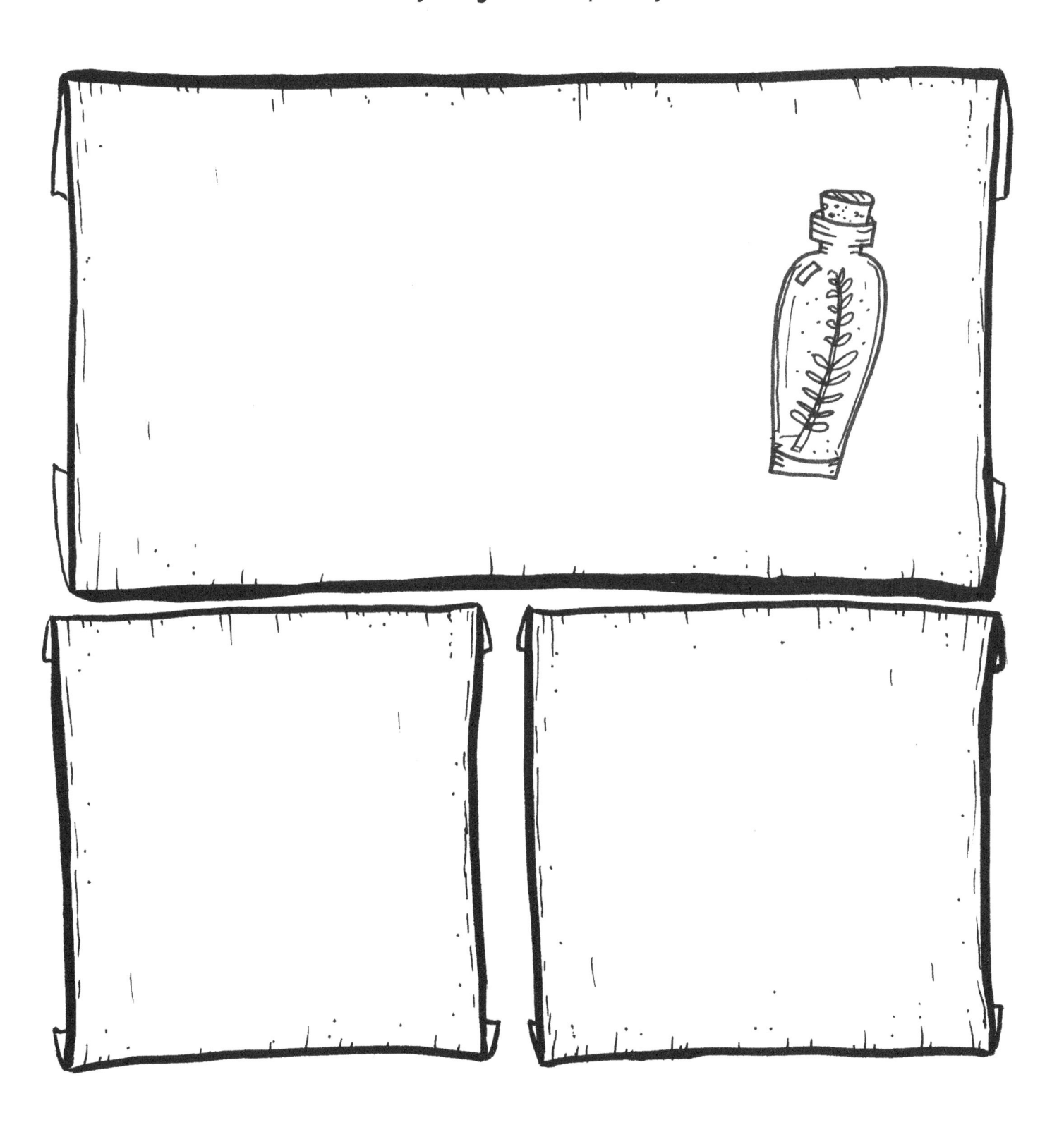

Plans & Priorities

Date:_____

To-do List:
_____
_____
_____
_____
_____

A Quote:
_____
_____
_____
_____

My Goals:
_____
_____
_____
_____

My Plans:
_____
_____
_____
_____

Notes:
_____
_____
_____

Relax & Be Creative

Drawing & Reading Time!

Choose a few books from your stack to focus on today.
Write down and draw what inspires you.
(Set a timer for 1 hour)

Study an Artist
From Portugal

Name:_____

What is this artist known for?
_____
_____
_____

What makes their artwork unique?
_____
_____
_____
_____
_____

Random fact about this artist or their art:
_____
_____

Write a short biography about this artist:
_____
_____
_____
_____
_____
_____
_____
_____
_____
_____
_____
_____

Design a postage stamp to commemorate this person

Screen Time

Watch a high-quality film, video, tutorial or documentary.

Title_____

Screen Time_____

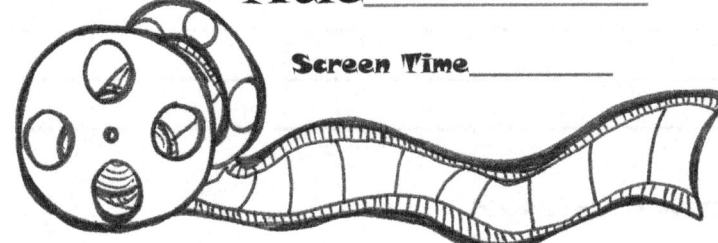

Producer_____

Actors_____
_____
_____
_____

Draw it

Pause the video and draw your favorite scene from the film.

Worst

Bad

Awful

Ok

Nice

Great

Best

Make a Comic

Based on the video you watched during screen time.

Title_____

Art Challenge

Draw your dream destination.

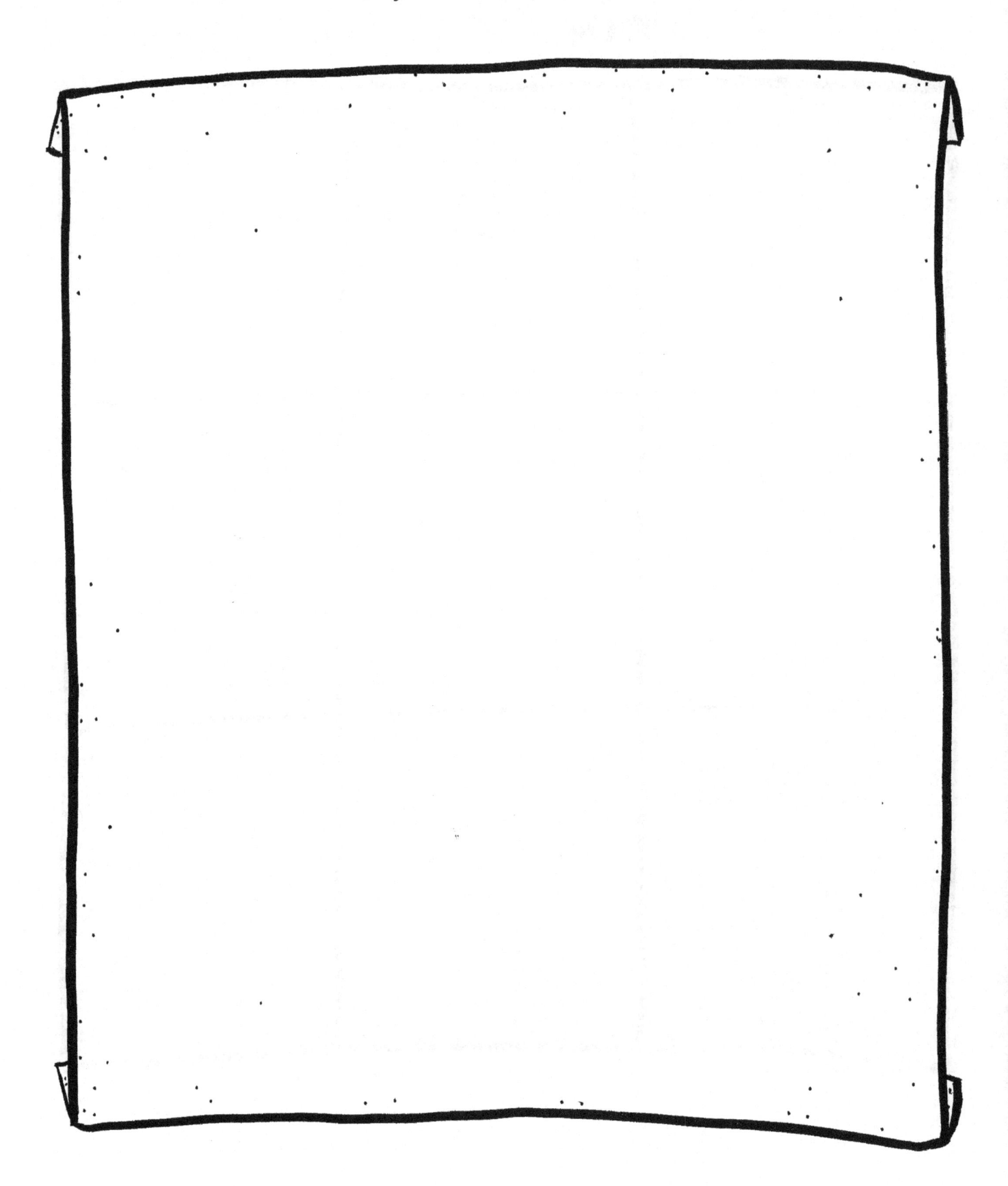

Math & Design Practice

Use this page for math practice, graphic design, pixel art, and creative measurements.

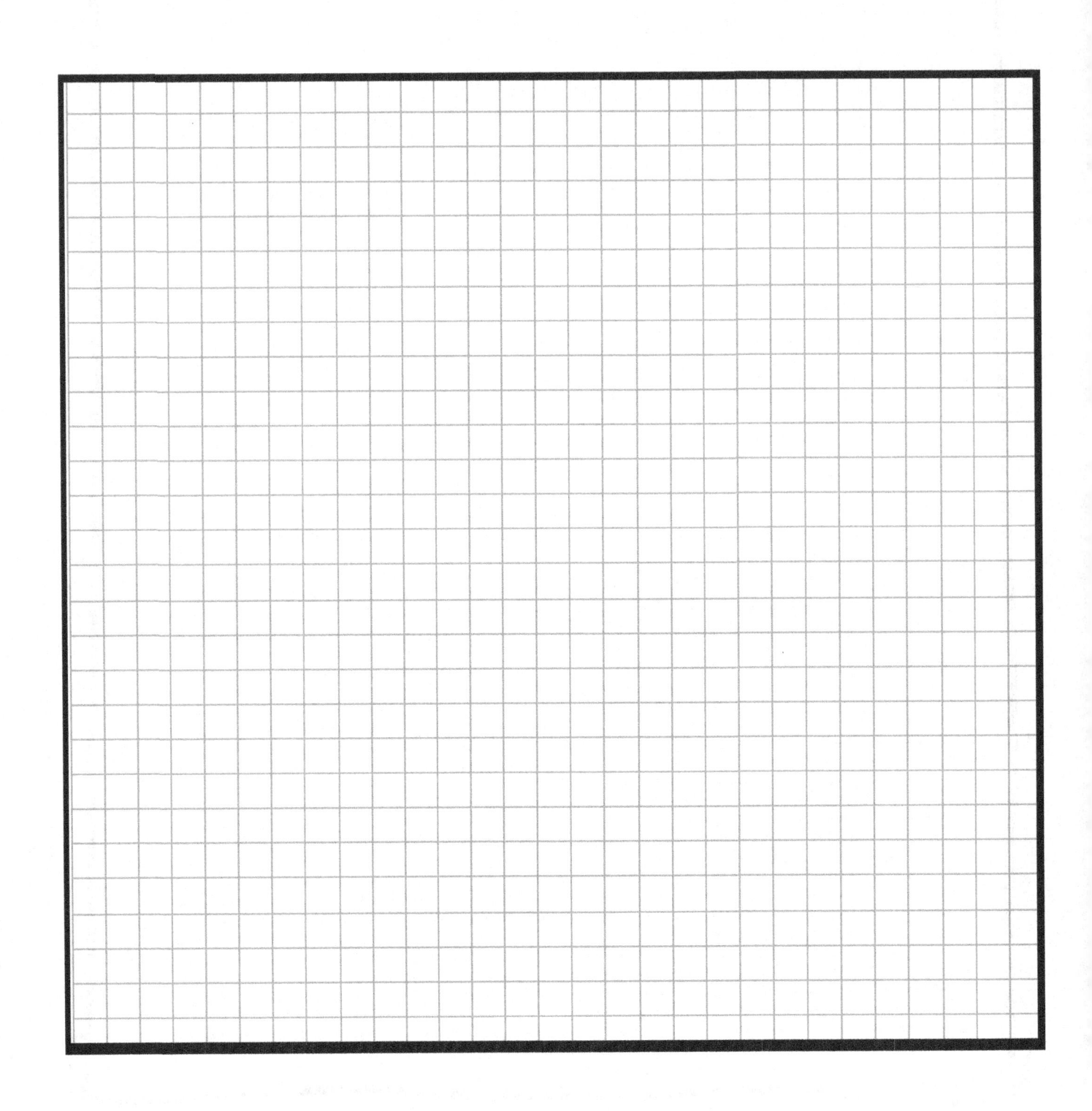

Nature Study

Take this book outside and draw anything and everything that inspires you.

Plans & Priorities

Date:_____

To-do List:
_____
_____
_____
_____
_____

A Quote:
_____
_____
_____
_____
_____

My Goals:
_____
_____
_____
_____
_____

My Plans:
_____
_____
_____
_____
_____

Notes:
_____
_____
_____
_____

Relax & Be Creative

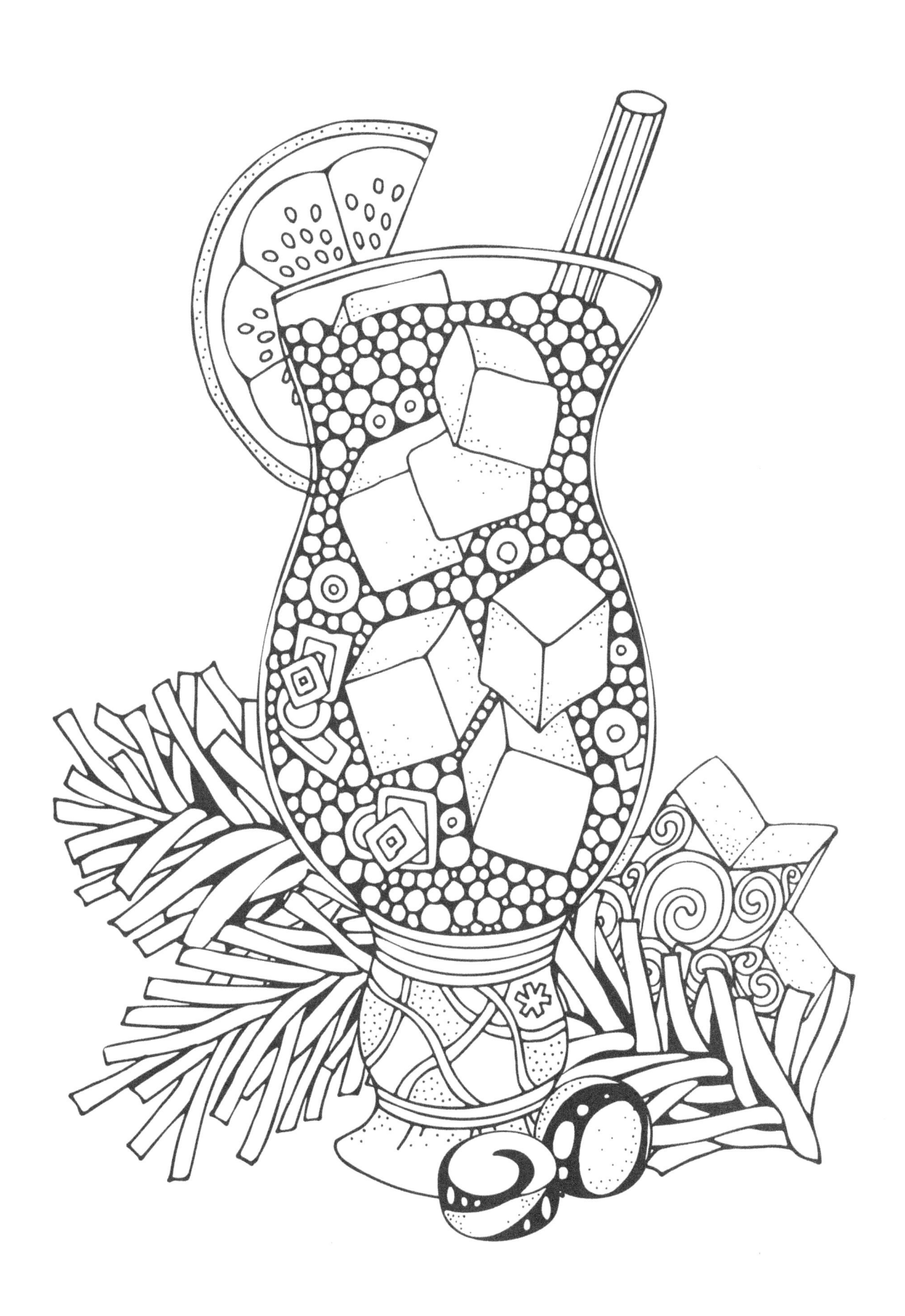

Drawing & Reading Time!

Choose a few books from your stack to focus on today.
Write down and draw what inspires you.
(Set a timer for 1 hour)

Study an Artist
You choose!

Name: _____

What is this artist known for?
_____
_____
_____

What makes their artwork unique?
_____
_____
_____
_____
_____

Random fact about this artist or their art:
_____
_____

Write a short biography about this artist:
_____
_____
_____
_____
_____
_____
_____
_____
_____
_____
_____
_____

Design a postage stamp to commemorate this person

Screen Time

Watch a high-quality film, video, tutorial or documentary.

Title_____

Screen Time_____

Producer_____

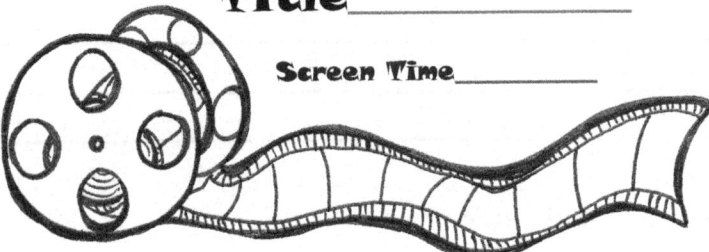

Actors_____

_____

_____

_____

Draw it

Pause the video and draw your favorite scene from the film.

Worst

Bad

Awful

Ok

Nice

Great

Best

Make a Comic

Based on the video you watched during screen time.

Title_____

Plans & Priorities

Date: _____

To-do List:
_____
_____
_____
_____

A Quote:
_____
_____
_____
_____

My Goals:
_____
_____
_____
_____

My Plans:
_____
_____
_____
_____

Notes:
_____
_____
_____
_____

Relax & Be Creative

Art Challenge

Draw a cafe in Paris.

Math & Design Practice

Use this page for math practice, graphic design, pixel art, and creative measurements.

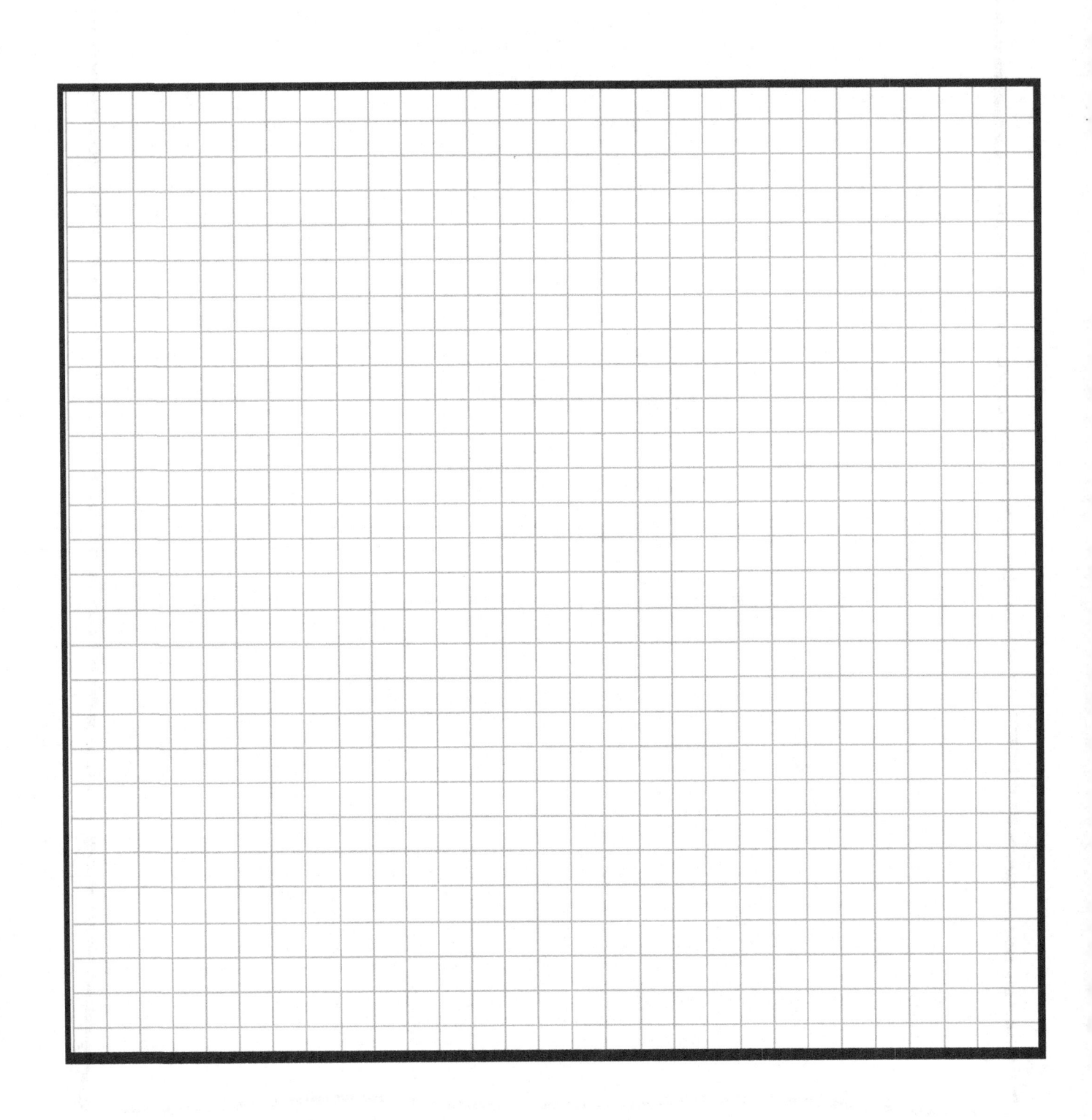

Nature Study

Take this book outside and draw anything and everything that inspires you.

Plans & Priorities

Date:_____

To-do List:
_____
_____
_____
_____
_____

A Quote:
_____
_____
_____
_____
_____

My Goals:
_____
_____
_____
_____

My Plans:
_____
_____
_____
_____

Notes:
_____
_____
_____
_____

Relax & Be Creative

Drawing & Reading Time!

Choose a few books from your stack to focus on today.
Write down and draw what inspires you.
(Set a timer for 1 hour)

Study an Artist
From India

Name: _____

What is this artist known for?
_____
_____
_____

What makes their artwork unique?
_____
_____
_____
_____
_____

Random fact about this artist or their art:
_____
_____

Write a short biography about this artist:
_____
_____
_____
_____
_____
_____
_____
_____
_____
_____
_____

Design a postage stamp to commemorate this person

Screen Time

Watch a high-quality film, video, tutorial or documentary.

Title_____

Screen Time_____

Producer_____

Actors_____

_____

_____

_____

Draw it

Pause the video and draw your favorite scene from the film.

Worst

Bad

Awful

Ok

Nice

Great

Best

Make a Comic

Based on the video you watched during screen time.

Title_____

Art Challenge

Draw what you think heaven might look like.

Math & Design Practice

Use this page for math practice, graphic design, pixel art, and creative measurements.

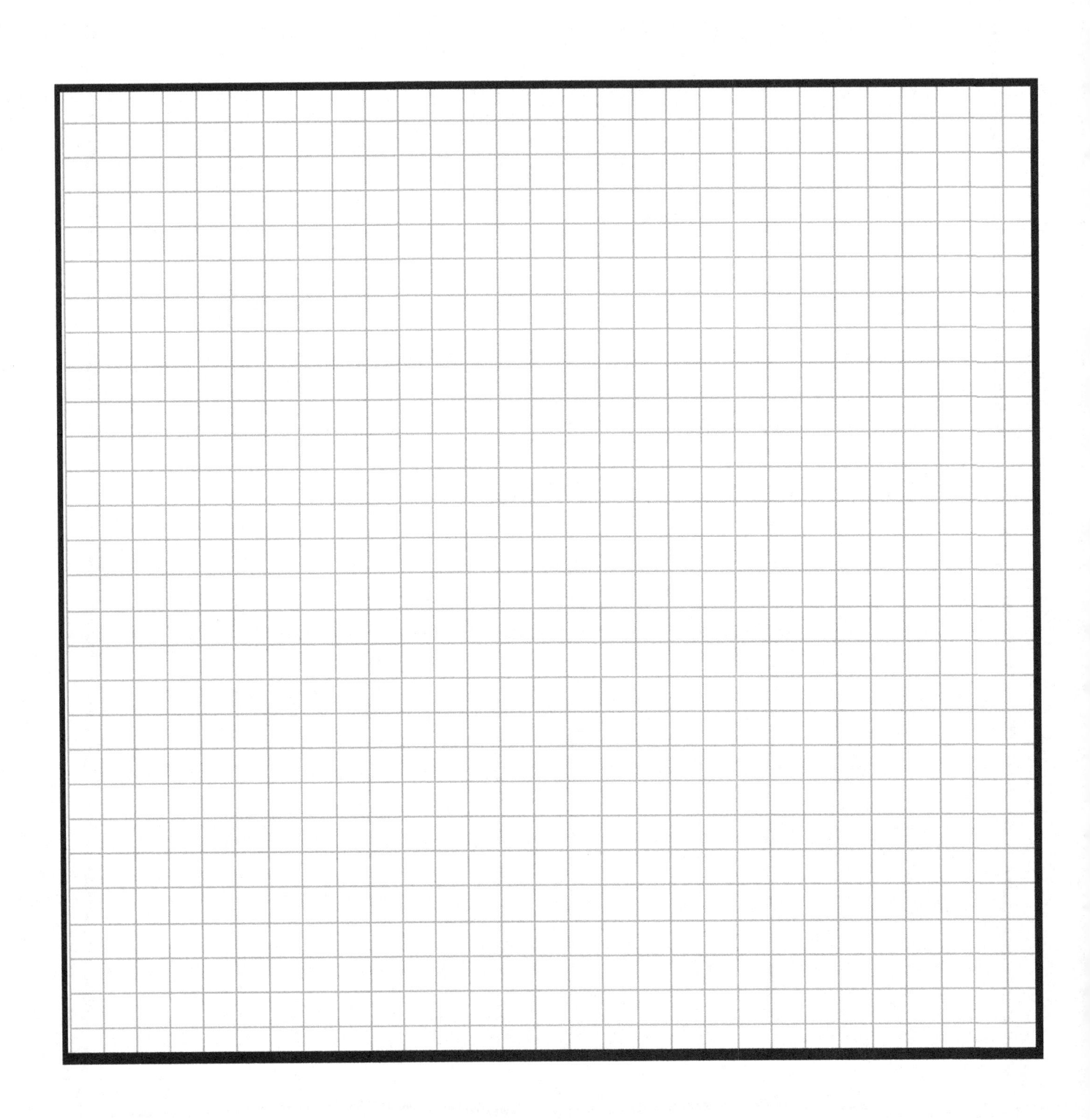

Nature Study

Take this book outside and draw anything and everything that inspires you.

Plans & Priorities

Date:_____

To-do List:
_____
_____
_____
_____
_____

A Quote:
_____
_____
_____
_____
_____

My Goals:
_____
_____
_____
_____
_____

My Plans:
_____
_____
_____
_____
_____

Notes:
_____
_____
_____
_____

Relax & Be Creative

Drawing & Reading Time!

Choose a few books from your stack to focus on today.
Write down and draw what inspires you.
(Set a timer for 1 hour)

Study an Artist
From Thailand

Name: _____

What is this artist known for?
_____
_____
_____

What makes their artwork unique?
_____
_____
_____
_____
_____

Random fact about this artist or their art:
_____
_____

Write a short biography about this artist:
_____
_____
_____
_____
_____
_____
_____
_____
_____
_____

Design a postage stamp to commemorate this person

Screen Time

Watch a high-quality film, video, tutorial or documentary.

Title_____

Screen Time_____

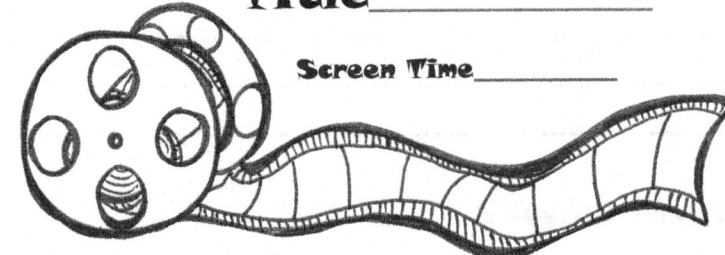

Producer_____
Actors_____
_____
_____
_____

Draw it

Pause the video and draw your favorite scene from the film.

Worst

Bad

Awful

Ok

Nice

Great

Best

Make a Comic

Based on the video you watched during screen time.

Title_____

Art Challenge

Draw a wedding.

Math & Design Practice

Use this page for math practice, graphic design, pixel art, and creative measurements.

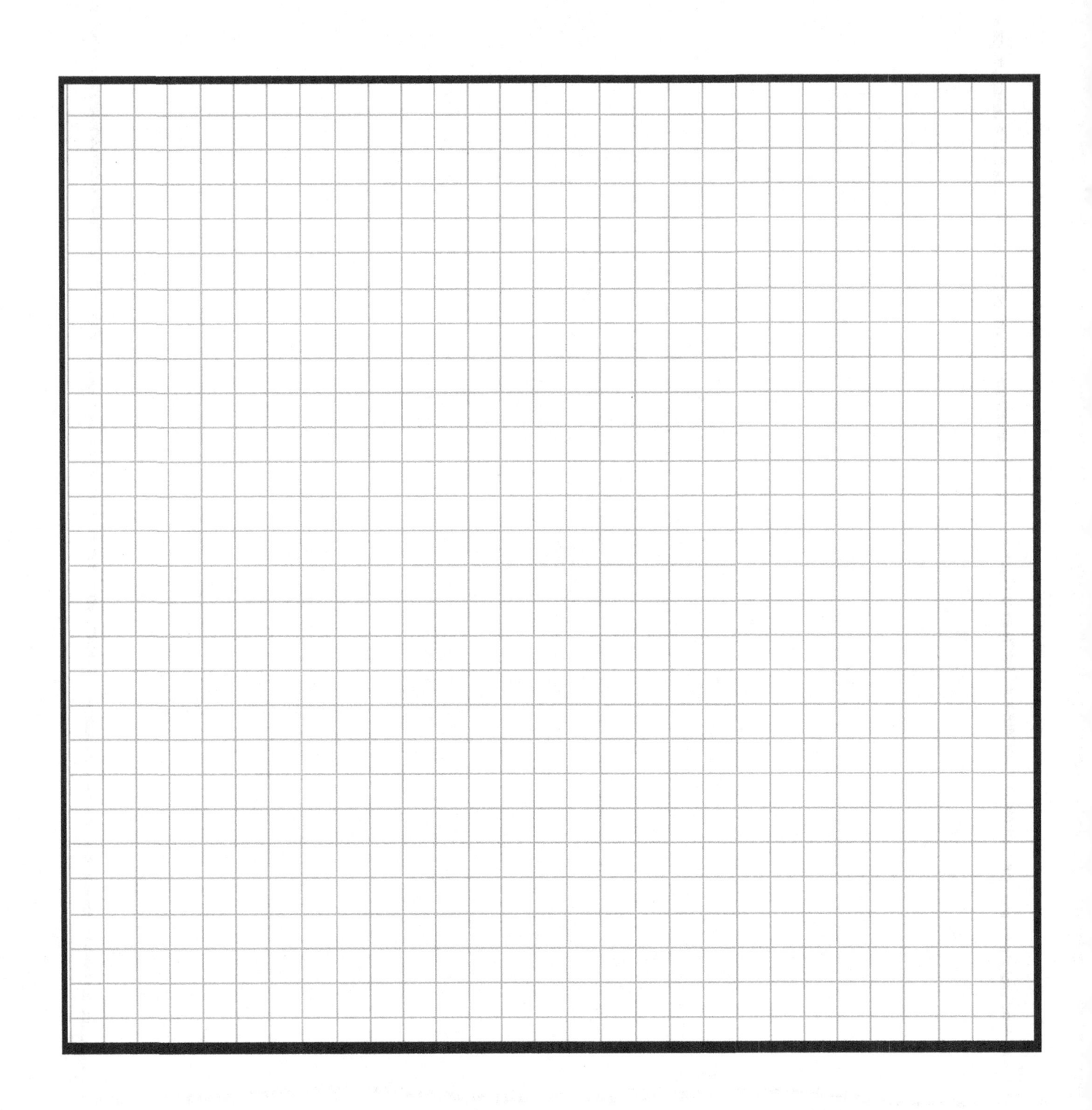

Nature Study

Take this book outside and draw anything and everything that inspires you.

Plans & Priorities

Date:_____

To-do List:
_____
_____
_____
_____
_____

A Quote:
_____
_____
_____
_____
_____

My Goals:
_____
_____
_____
_____
_____

My Plans:
_____
_____
_____
_____
_____

Notes:
_____
_____
_____
_____

Relax & Be Creative

Drawing & Reading Time!

Choose a few books from your stack to focus on today.
Write down and draw what inspires you.
(Set a timer for 1 hour)

Study an Artist
From the 1900's

Name:_____

What is this artist known for?
_____
_____
_____

What makes their artwork unique?
_____
_____
_____
_____
_____

Random fact about this artist or their art:
_____
_____

Write a short biography about this artist:
_____
_____
_____
_____
_____
_____
_____
_____
_____
_____
_____
_____

Design a postage stamp to commemorate this person

Screen Time

Watch a high-quality film, video, tutorial or documentary.

Title_____

Screen Time_____

Producer_____

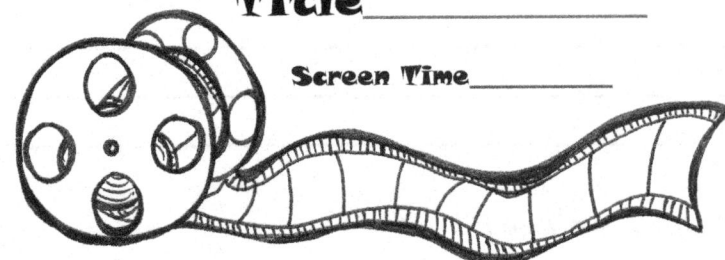

Actors_____

_____
_____
_____

Draw it

Pause the video and draw your favorite scene from the film.

Worst

Bad

Awful

Ok

Nice

Great

Best

Make a Comic

Based on the video you watched during screen time.

Title _____

Art Challenge

Draw bravery.

Math & Design Practice

Use this page for math practice, graphic design, pixel art, and creative measurements.

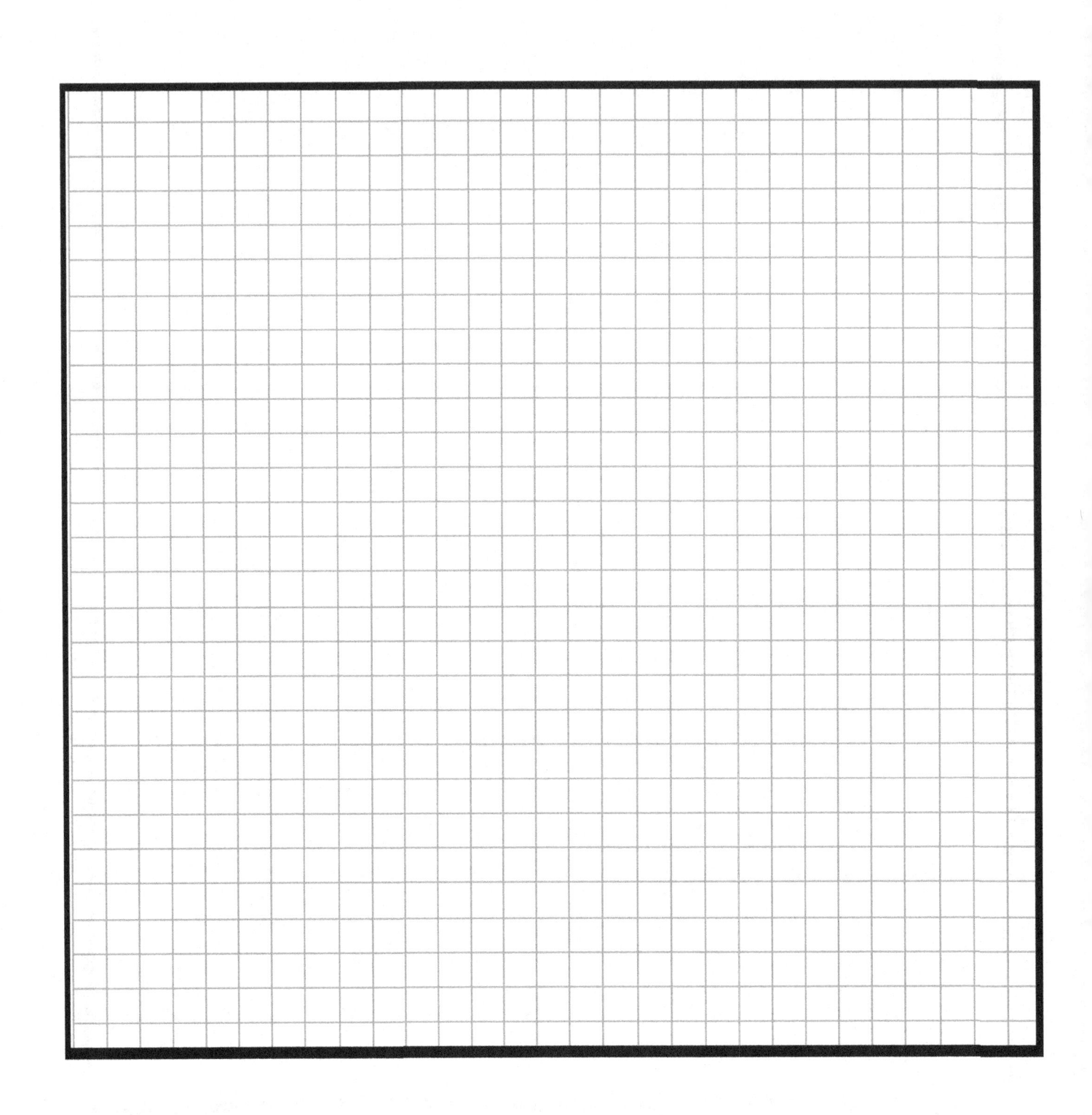

Nature Study

Take this book outside and draw anything and everything that inspires you.

Plans & Priorities

Date:_____

To-do List:
_____
_____
_____
_____

A Quote:
_____
_____
_____
_____

My Goals:
_____
_____
_____
_____
_____

My Plans:
_____
_____
_____
_____

Notes:
_____
_____
_____
_____

Relax & Be Creative

Drawing & Reading Time!

Choose a few books from your stack to focus on today.
Write down and draw what inspires you.
(Set a timer for 1 hour)

Study an Artist
From Japan

Name:_____

What is this artist known for?
_____
_____
_____

What makes their artwork unique?
_____
_____
_____
_____
_____

Random fact about this artist or their art:
_____
_____

Write a short biography about this artist:
_____
_____
_____
_____
_____
_____
_____
_____
_____
_____
_____
_____

Design a postage stamp to commemorate this person

Screen Time

Watch a high-quality film, video, tutorial or documentary.

Title_____

Screen Time_____

Producer_____

Actors_____

_____

_____

_____

Draw it

Pause the video and draw your favorite scene from the film.

Worst

Bad

Awful

Ok

Nice

Great

Best

Make a Comic

Based on the video you watched during screen time.

Title_____

Art Challenge

Draw a dancer.

Math & Design Practice

Use this page for math practice, graphic design, pixel art, and creative measurements.

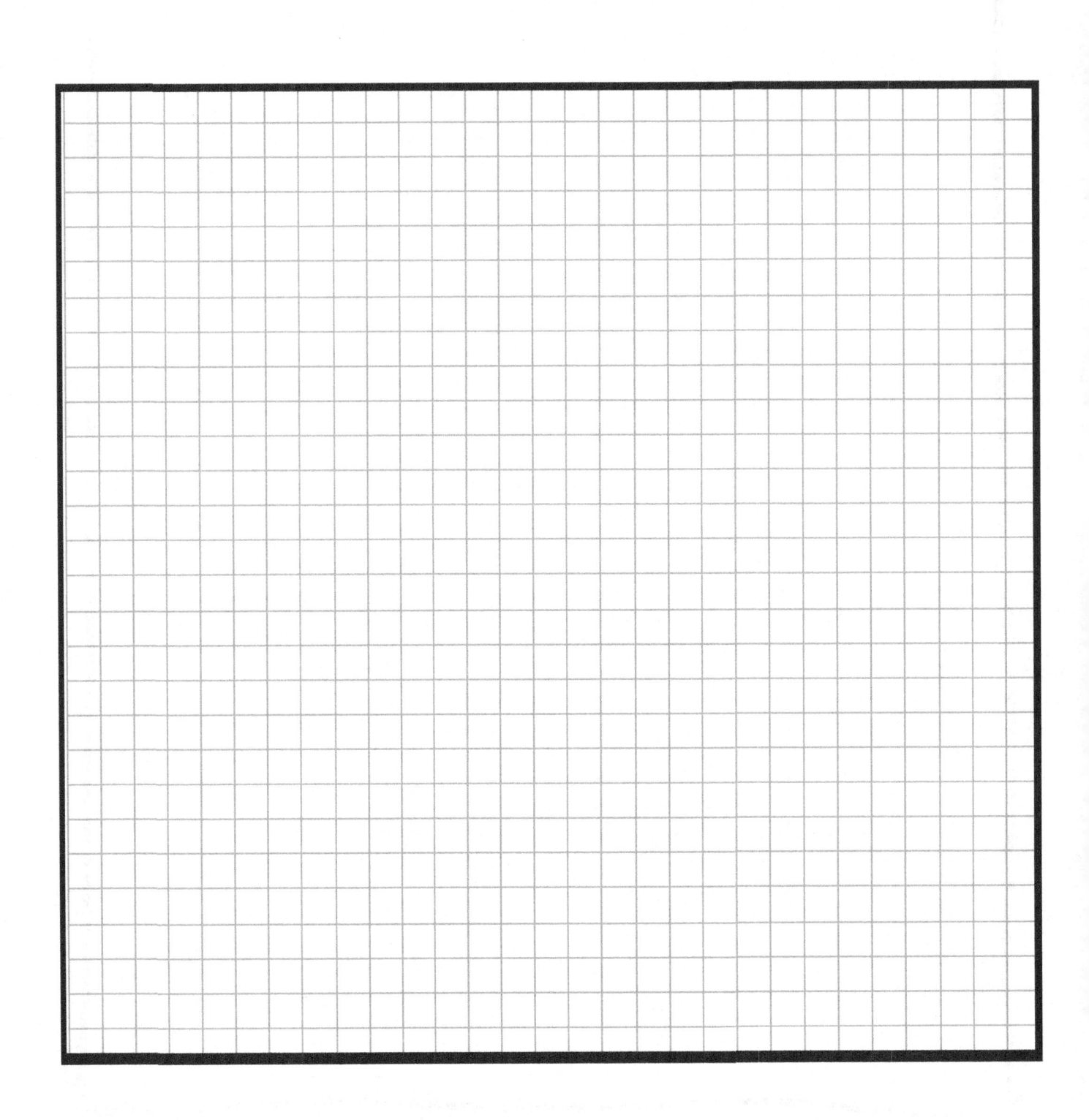

Nature Study

Take this book outside and draw anything and everything that inspires you.

Plans & Priorities

Date:_____

To-do List:
_____
_____
_____
_____
_____

A Quote:
_____
_____
_____
_____

My Goals:
_____
_____
_____
_____

My Plans:
_____
_____
_____
_____

Notes:
_____
_____
_____
_____

Relax & Be Creative

Drawing & Reading Time!

Choose a few books from your stack to focus on today.
Write down and draw what inspires you.
(Set a timer for 1 hour)

Study an Artist
From Austria

Name:_____

What is this artist known for?
_____
_____
_____

What makes their artwork unique?
_____
_____
_____
_____
_____

Random fact about this artist or their art:
_____
_____

Write a short biography about this artist:
_____
_____
_____
_____
_____
_____
_____
_____
_____
_____
_____
_____

Design a postage stamp to commemorate this person

Screen Time

Watch a high-quality film, video, tutorial or documentary.

Title_____

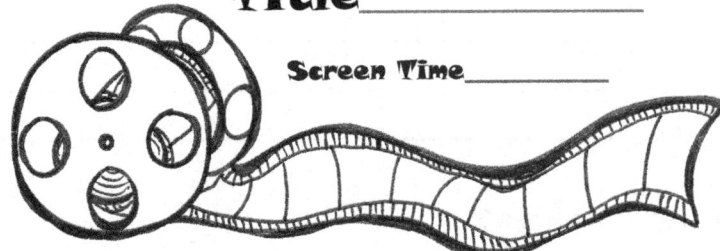

Screen Time_____

Producer_____

Actors_____

_____

_____

_____

Draw it

Pause the video and draw your favorite scene from the film.

Worst

Bad

Awful

Ok

Nice

Great

Best

Make a Comic

Based on the video you watched during screen time.

Title_____

Art Challenge

Draw love.

Math & Design Practice

Use this page for math practice, graphic design, pixel art, and creative measurements.

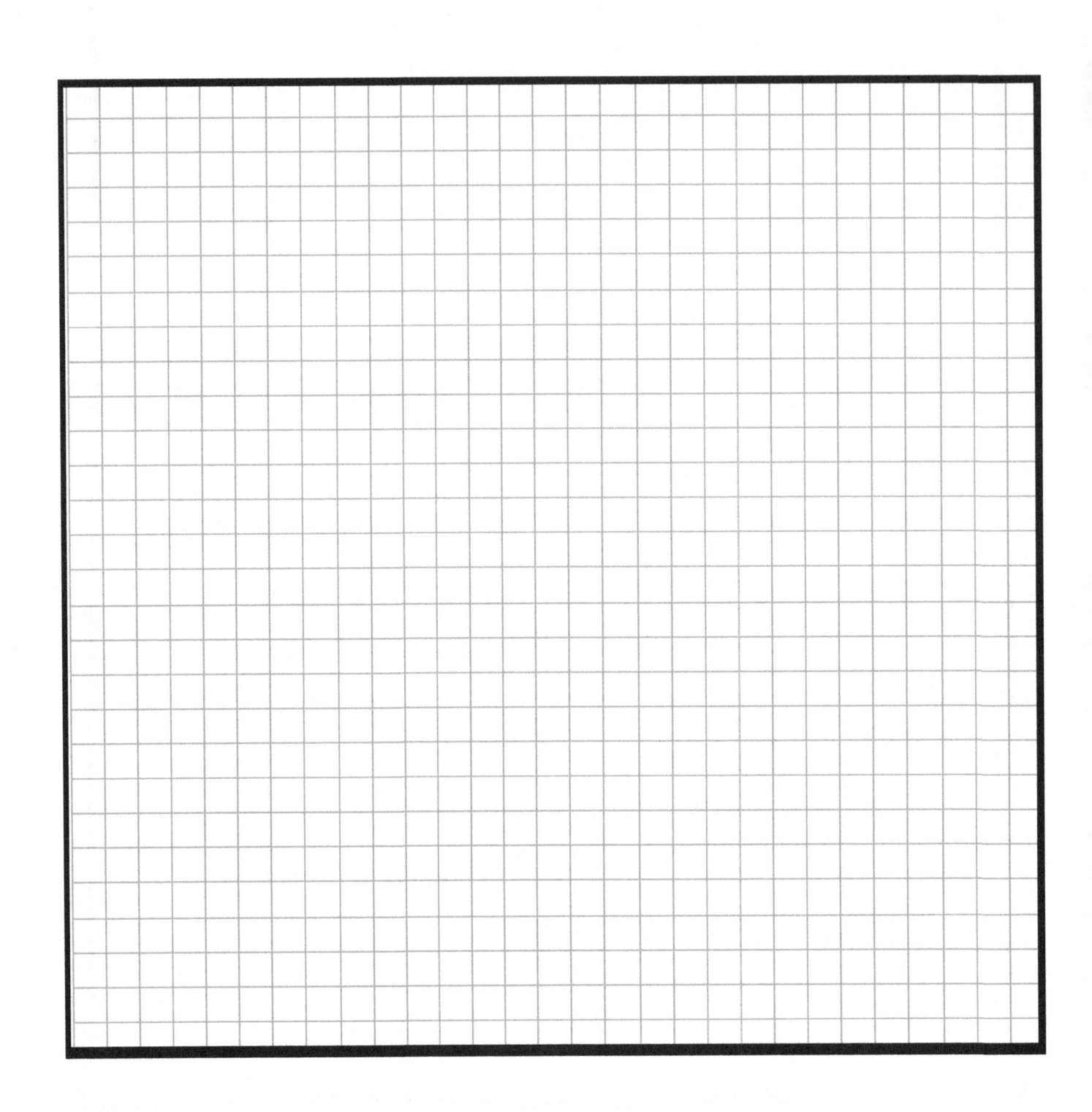

Nature Study

Take this book outside and draw anything and everything that inspires you.

Plans & Priorities

Date:_____

To-do List:
_____
_____
_____
_____

A Quote:
_____
_____
_____
_____

My Goals:
_____
_____
_____
_____

My Plans:
_____
_____
_____
_____

Notes:
_____
_____
_____
_____

Relax & Be Creative

Drawing & Reading Time!

Choose a few books from your stack to focus on today.
Write down and draw what inspires you.
(Set a timer for 1 hour)

Study an Artist
You choose!

Name: _____

What is this artist known for?
_____
_____
_____

What makes their artwork unique?
_____
_____
_____
_____
_____
_____

Random fact about this artist or their art:
_____
_____

Write a short biography about this artist:
_____
_____
_____
_____
_____
_____
_____
_____
_____
_____
_____
_____

Design a postage stamp to commemorate this person

Screen Time

Watch a high-quality film, video, tutorial or documentary.

Title_____

Screen Time_____

Producer_____

Actors_____
_____
_____
_____
_____

Draw it

Pause the video and draw your favorite scene from the film.

Worst

Bad

Awful

Ok

Nice

Great

Best

Make a Comic

Based on the video you watched during screen time.

Title_____

Art Challenge

Copy a drawing by your favorite artist.

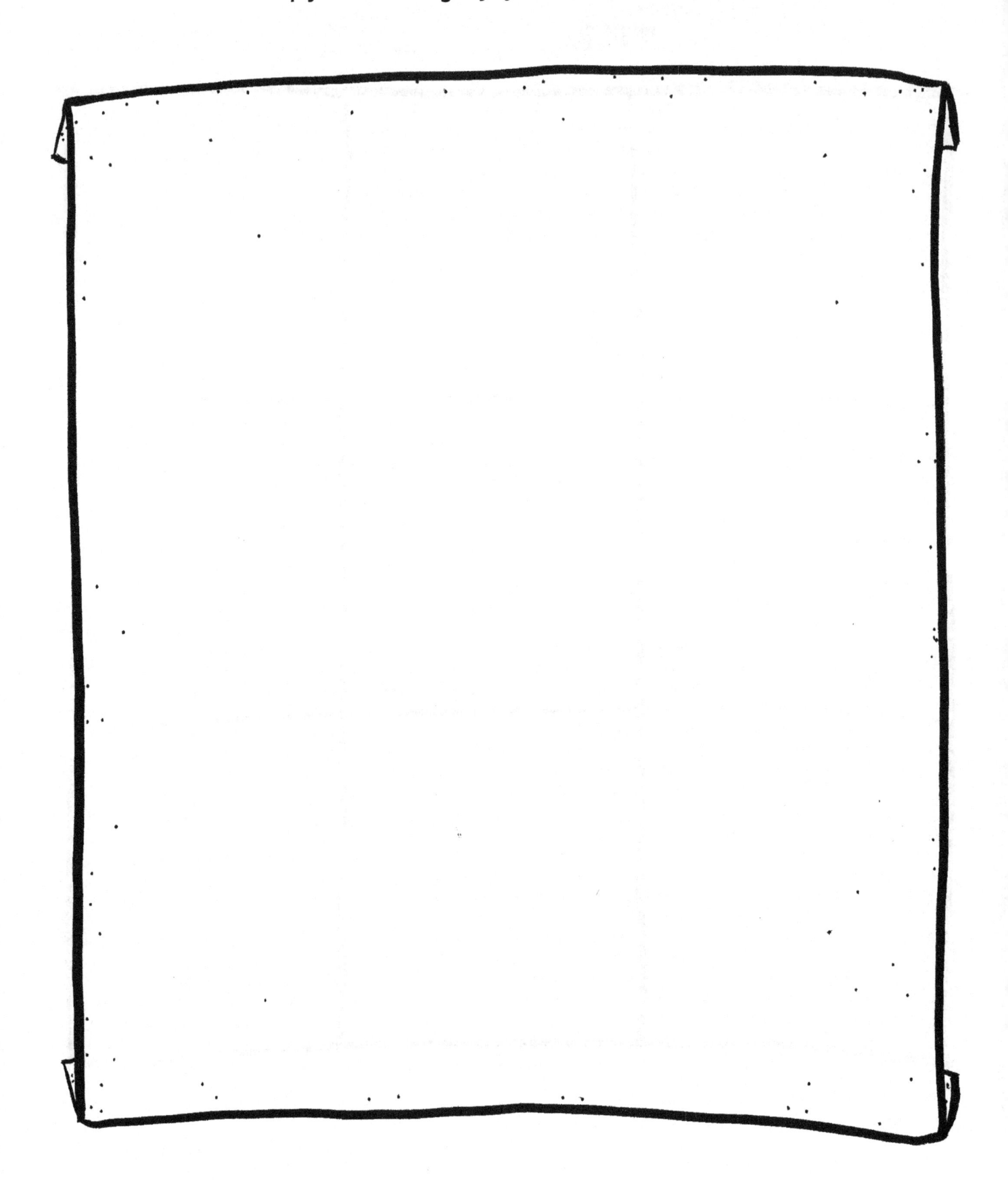

Math & Design Practice

Use this page for math practice, graphic design, pixel art, and creative measurements.

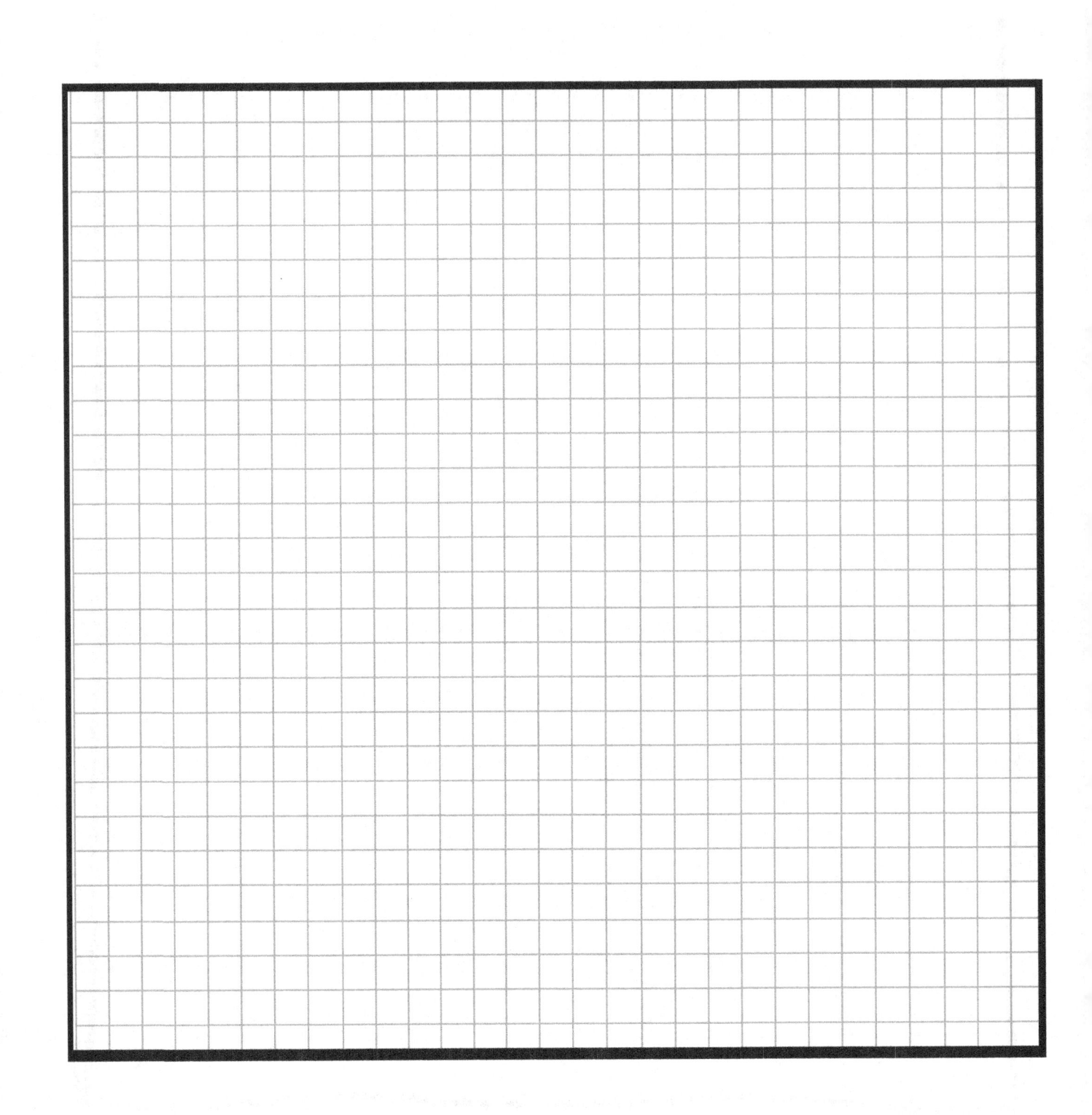

Nature Study

Take this book outside and draw anything and everything that inspires you.

Plans & Priorities

Date: _____

To-do List:
_____
_____
_____
_____
_____

A Quote:
_____
_____
_____
_____

My Goals:
_____
_____
_____
_____

My Plans:
_____
_____
_____
_____

Notes:
_____
_____
_____
_____

Relax & Be Creative

Drawing & Reading Time!

Choose a few books from your stack to focus on today.
Write down and draw what inspires you.
(Set a timer for 1 hour)

Study an Artist
From Australia

Name: _____

What is this artist known for?
_____
_____
_____

What makes their artwork unique?
_____
_____
_____
_____
_____

Random fact about this artist or their art:
_____
_____

Write a short biography about this artist:
_____
_____
_____
_____
_____
_____
_____
_____
_____
_____
_____
_____

Design a postage stamp to commemorate this person

Screen Time

Watch a high-quality film, video, tutorial or documentary.

Title_____

Screen Time_____

Producer_____

Actors_____
_____
_____
_____
_____

Draw it

Pause the video and draw your favorite scene from the film.

Worst

Bad

Awful

Ok

Nice

Great

Best

Make a Comic

Based on the video you watched during screen time.

Title_____

Art Challenge

Draw a rainy day and a stormy night.

Math & Design Practice

Use this page for math practice, graphic design, pixel art, and creative measurements.

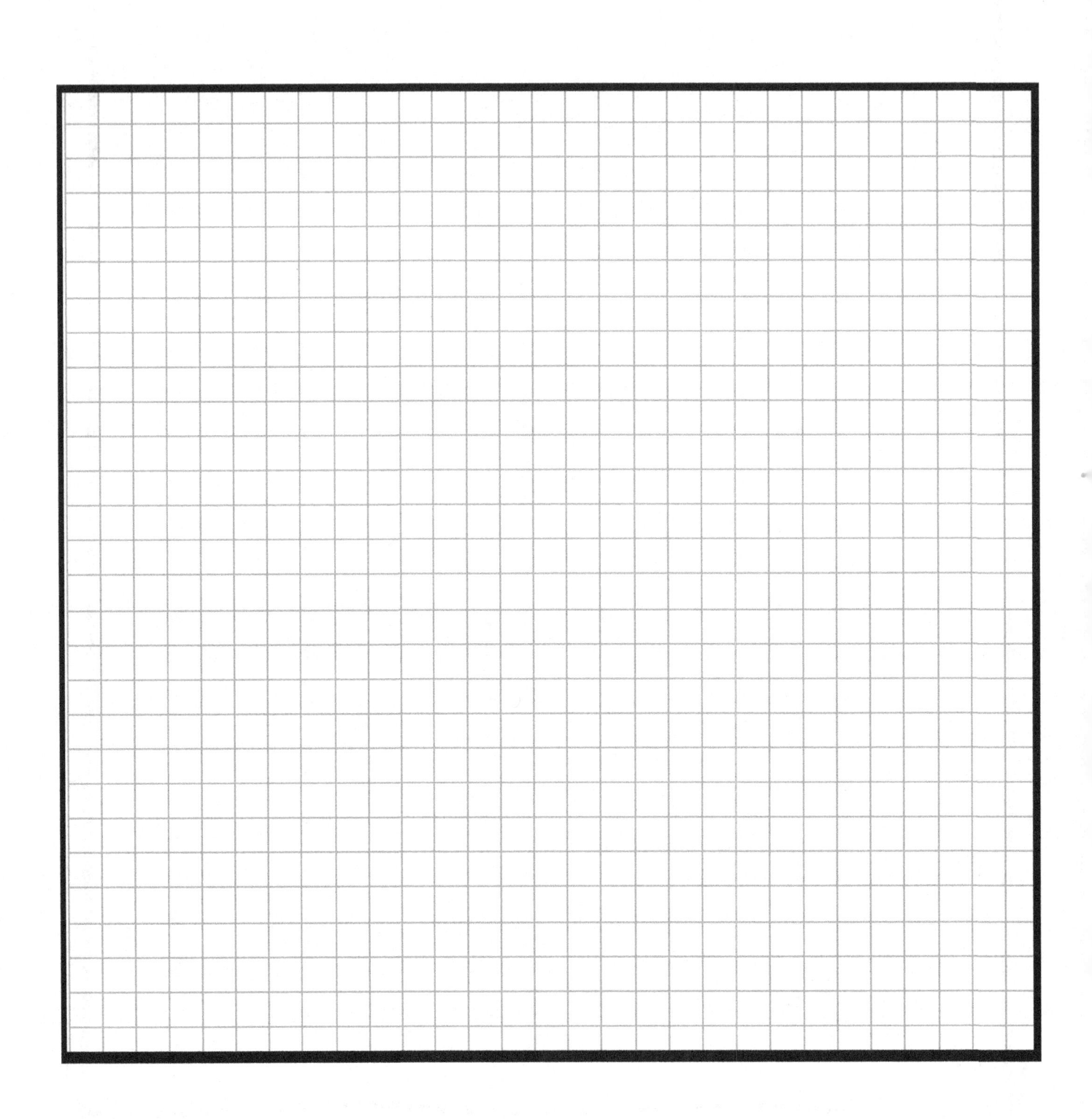

Nature Study

Take this book outside and draw anything and everything that inspires you.

Plans & Priorities

Date: _____

To-do List:
_____
_____
_____
_____
_____

A Quote:
_____
_____
_____
_____
_____

My Goals:
_____
_____
_____
_____
_____

My Plans:
_____
_____
_____
_____
_____

Notes:
_____
_____
_____
_____

Relax & Be Creative

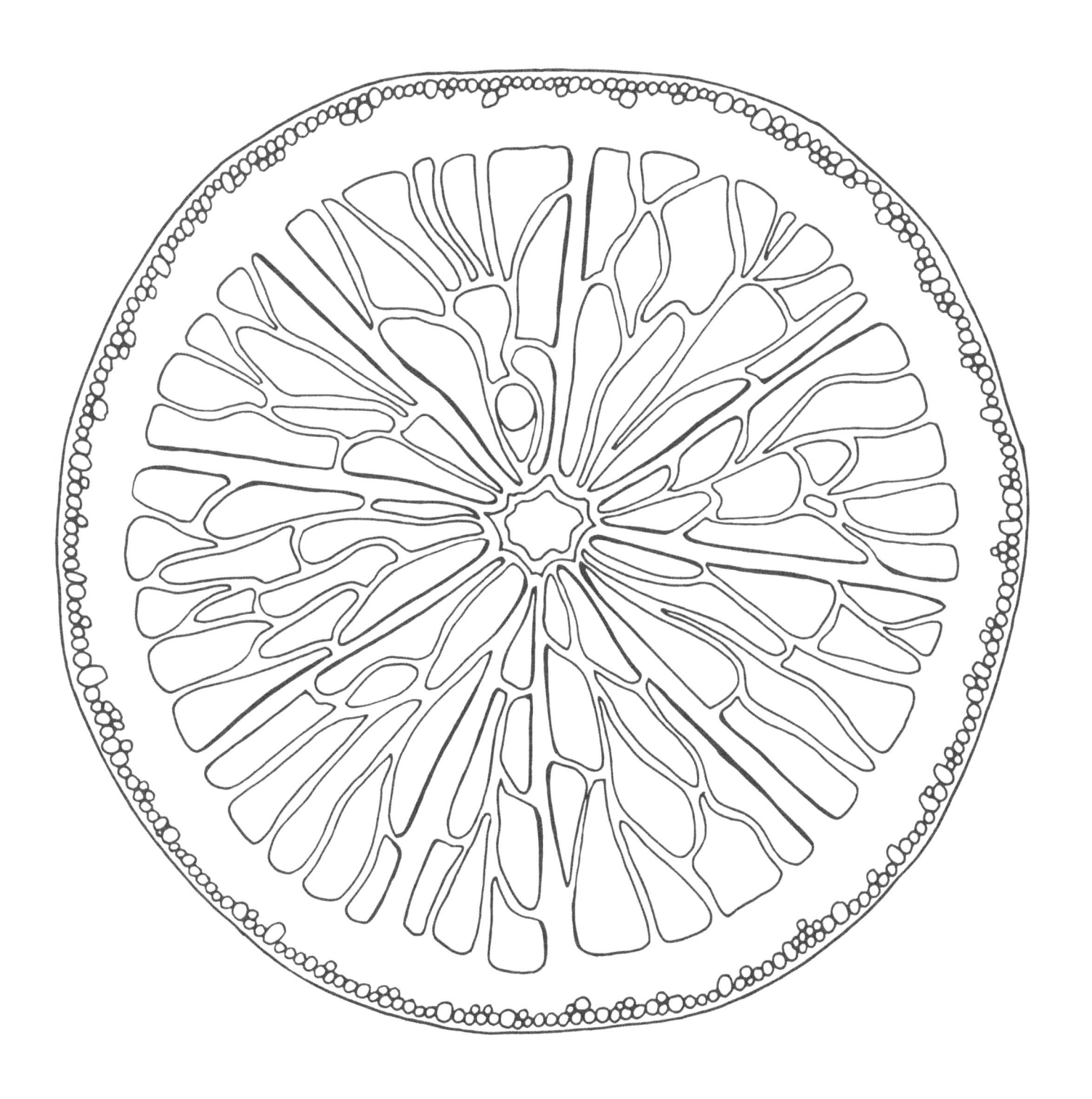

Drawing & Reading Time!

Choose a few books from your stack to focus on today.
Write down and draw what inspires you.
(Set a timer for 1 hour)

Study an Artist
From Iceland

Name:_____

What is this artist known for?
_____
_____
_____

What makes their artwork unique?
_____
_____
_____
_____
_____

Random fact about this artist or their art:
_____
_____

Write a short biography about this artist:
_____
_____
_____
_____
_____
_____
_____
_____
_____
_____
_____

Design a postage stamp to commemorate this person

Screen Time

Watch a high-quality film, video, tutorial or documentary.

Title_____

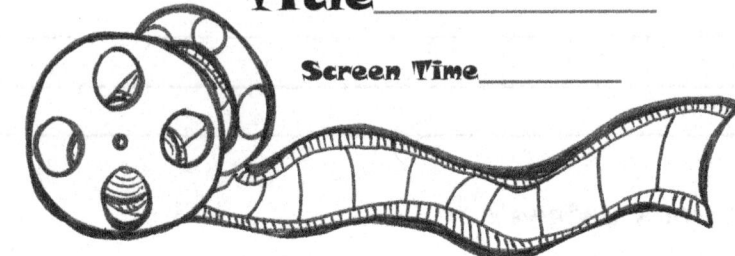

Screen Time_____

Producer_____

Actors_____
_____
_____
_____

Draw it

Pause the video and draw your favorite scene from the film.

Worst

Bad

Awful

Ok

Nice

Great

Best

Make a Comic

Based on the video you watched during screen time.

Title_____

Art Challenge

Draw a winter day and summer day.

Math & Design Practice

Use this page for math practice, graphic design, pixel art, and creative measurements.

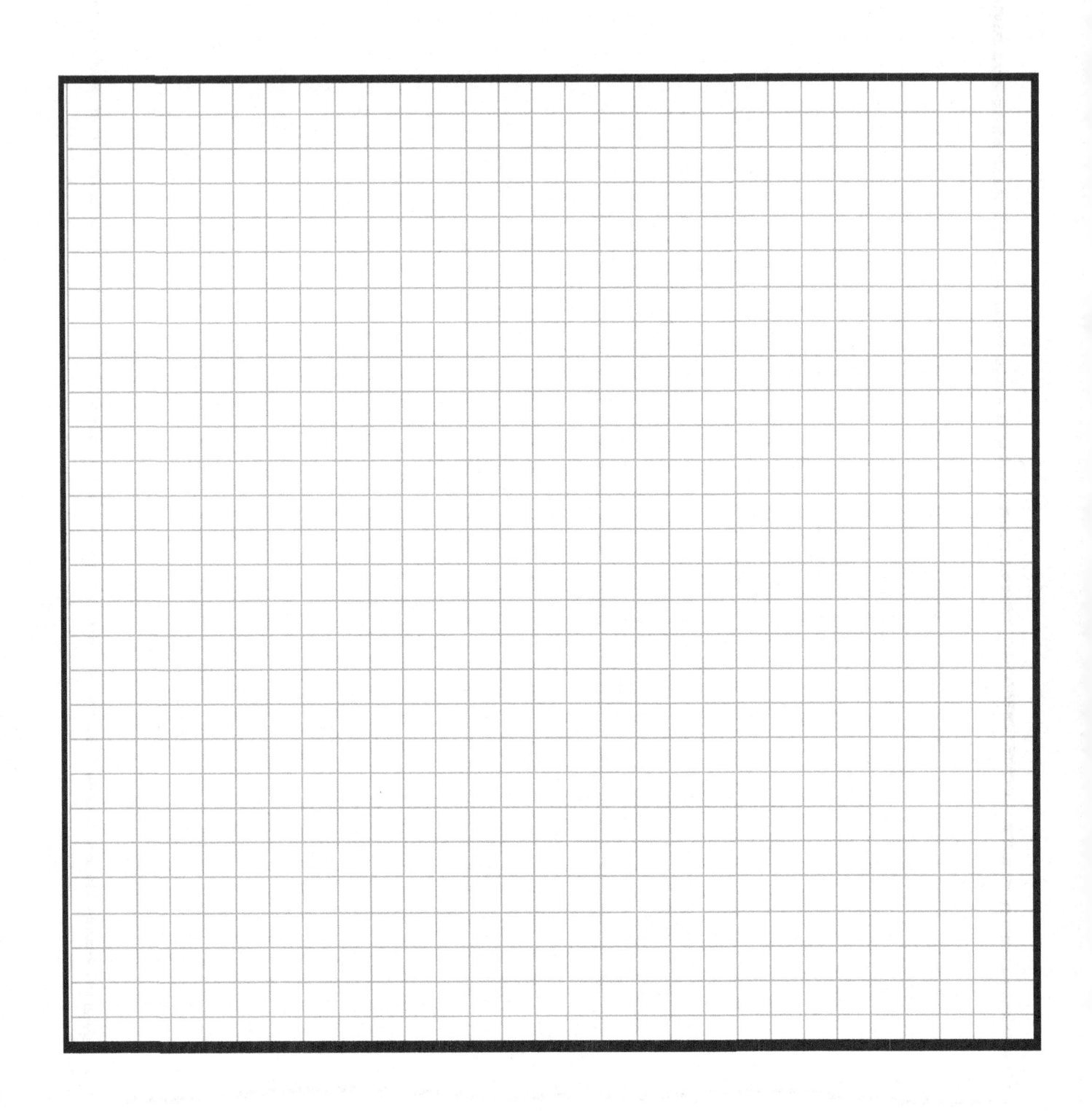

Nature Study

Take this book outside and draw anything and everything that inspires you.

Plans & Priorities

Date:_____

To-do List:
_____
_____
_____
_____
_____

A Quote:
_____
_____
_____
_____

My Goals:
_____
_____
_____
_____

My Plans:
_____
_____
_____
_____

Notes:
_____
_____
_____
_____

Relax & Be Creative

Drawing & Reading Time!

Choose a few books from your stack to focus on today.
Write down and draw what inspires you.
(Set a timer for 1 hour)

Study an Artist
From Hungary

Name: _____

What is this artist known for?
_____
_____
_____

What makes their artwork unique?
_____
_____
_____
_____
_____

Random fact about this artist or their art:
_____
_____

Write a short biography about this artist:
_____
_____
_____
_____
_____
_____
_____
_____
_____
_____
_____

Design a postage stamp to commemorate this person

Screen Time

Watch a high-quality film, video, tutorial or documentary.

Title_____

Screen Time_____

Producer_____
Actors_____
_____
_____
_____

Draw it

Pause the video and draw your favorite scene from the film.

Worst

Bad

Awful

Ok

Nice

Great

Best

Make a Comic

Based on the video you watched during screen time.

Title_____

Art Challenge

Draw something in the room you are in. Use your left hand if you are right handed, or your right hand if you are left handed.

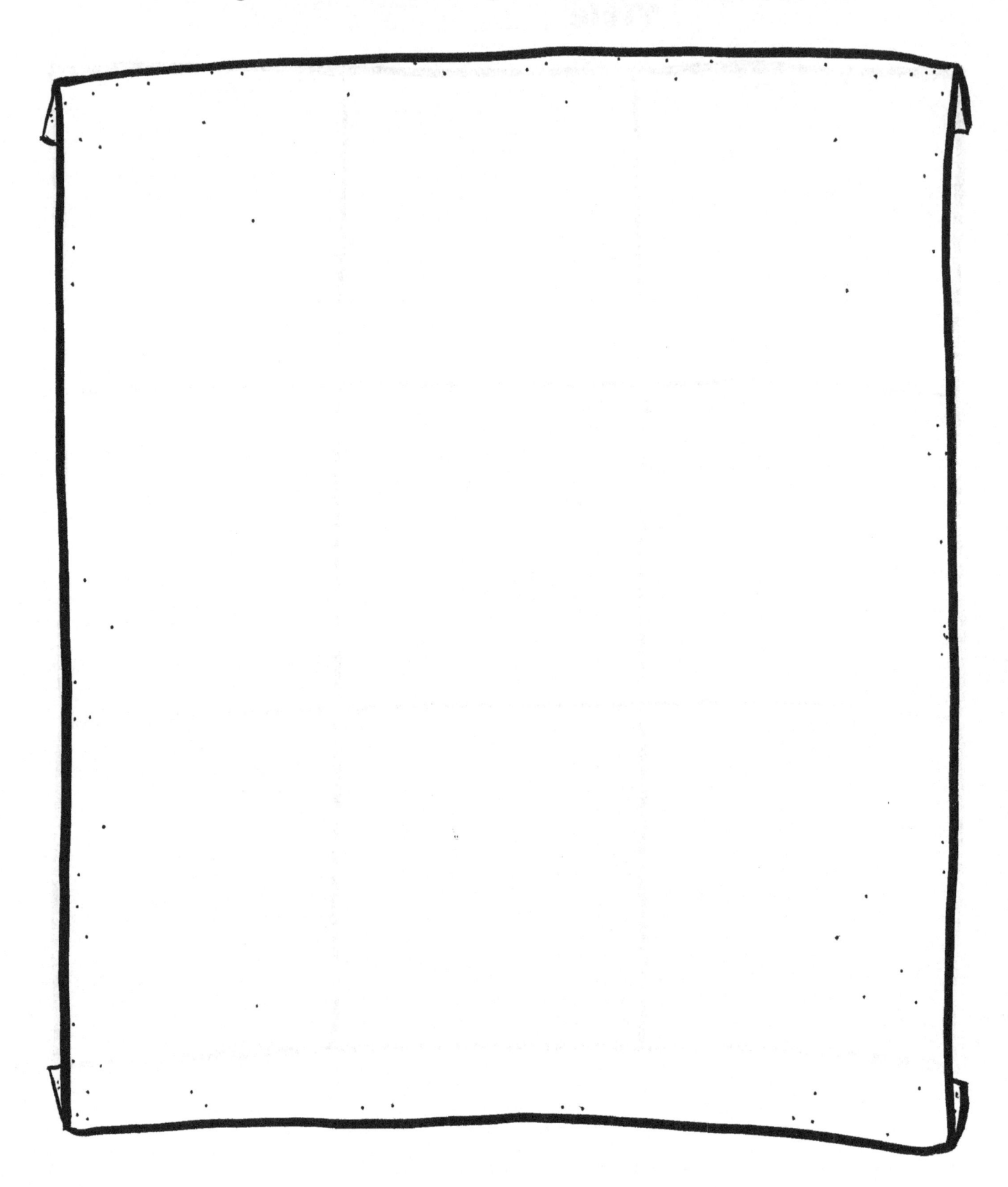

Math & Design Practice

Use this page for math practice, graphic design, pixel art, and creative measurements.

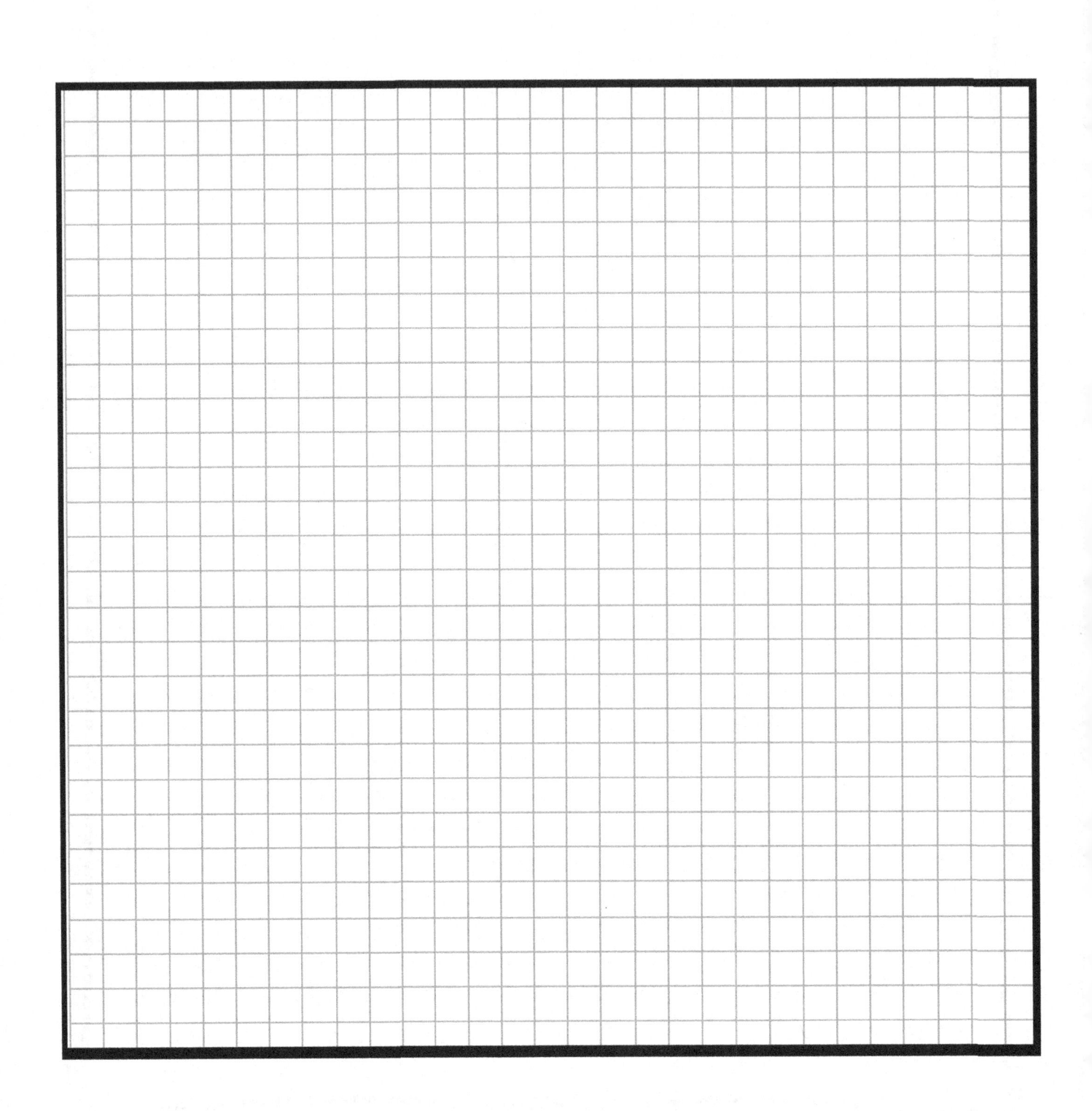

Nature Study

Take this book outside and draw anything and everything that inspires you.

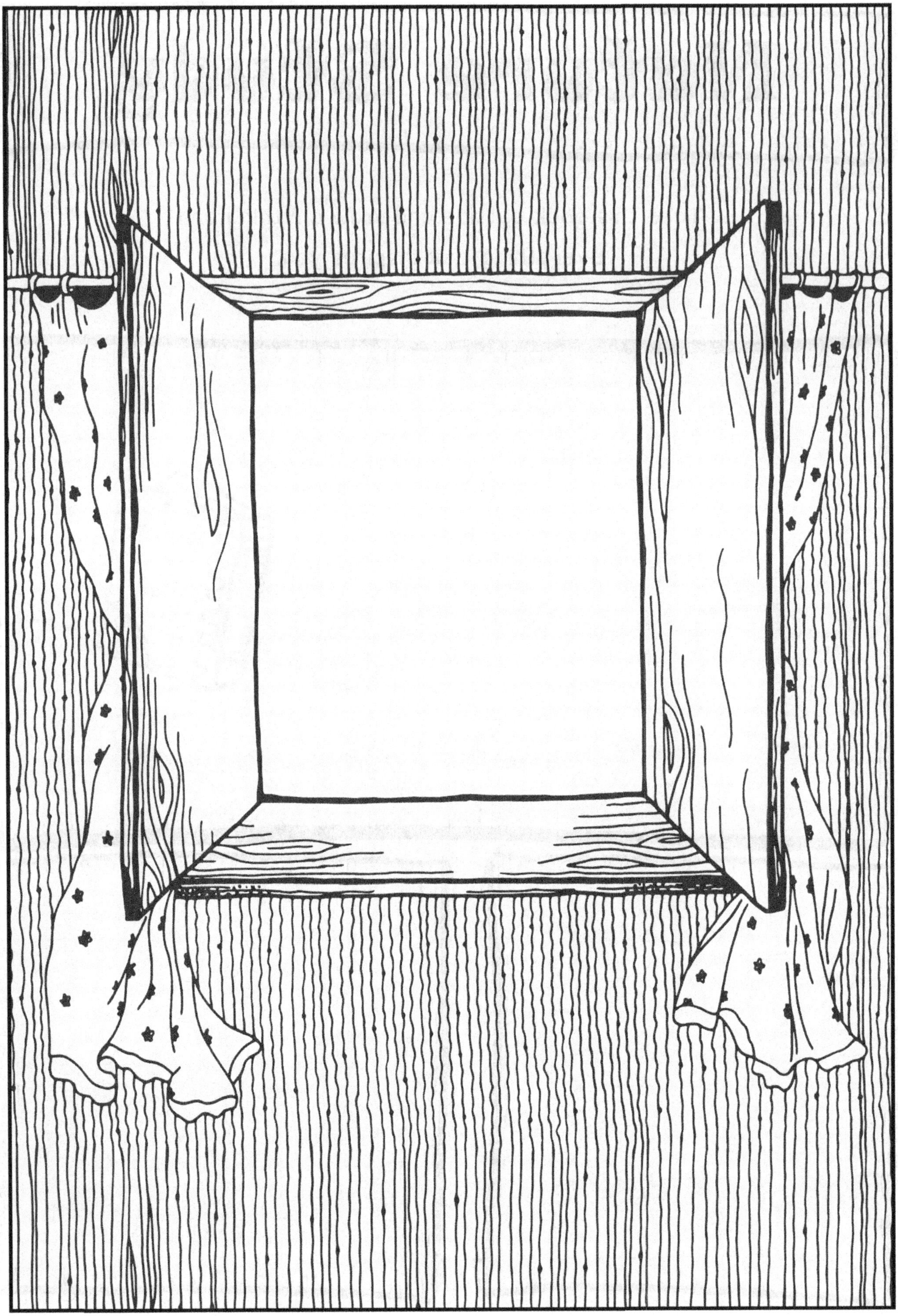

What Is Fun-Schooling?

Fun-schooling is a one-of-a-kind way to learn. It is tapping into kids interests while covering all the major subjects. Fun-schooling is for creative learners, students with learning disabilities, gifted students, and everyone in between. It's a way for students to learn without the stress, pressure, and boredom of other methods. We started out creating materials for our children. Then friends and family wanted to try it out. Before we knew it, Fun-schooling with Thinking Tree Books was born!

Fun-Schooling With Thinking Tree Books

Copyright Information

Thinking Tree Fun-Schooling Books, and electronic printable downloads are for home and family use only. You may make copies of these materials for only the children in your household.

All other uses of this material must be permitted in writing by Thinking Tree LLC. It is a violation of copyright law to distribute the electronic files or make copies for your friends, associates or students without. For information on using these materials for businesses, co-ops, summer camps, day camps, daycare, afterschool program, churches, or schools please contact us for licensing.

Contact Us:

The Thinking Tree LLC

+1 (USA)   317.622.8852

info@funschooling.com

Learn more about Fun-Schooling at:

FunSchooling.com

THE Thinking TREE
PUBLISHING COMPANY
ART
LOGIC
SCIENCE
SPELLING
READING
COLORING
THINKING
DRAWING
CREATING
Sarah Janisse Brown

Made in the USA
Coppell, TX
24 August 2024

36379872R00168